GW01238894

Spring Baby

A Christian Experience of
Infertility and IVF

Rebecca Baxter

Copyright © 2014 Rebecca Baxter

All rights reserved.

ISBN-13: 978-1497314689

ISBN-10: 1497314682

THE HOLY BIBLE, NEW INTERNATIONAL VERSION®, NIV® Copyright
© 1973, 1978, 1984, 2011 by Biblica, Inc.®
Used by permission. All rights reserved worldwide.

Good News Bible © 1994 published by the Bible Societies/HarperCollins
Publishers Ltd UK, Good News Bible© American Bible Society 1966, 1971, 1976,
1992. Used with permission

DEDICATION

To Mum, with much love

ACKNOWLEDGMENTS

Thank you to all those who have helped us
on our journey in so many different ways,
spiritually, socially and medically.

Author's Note

Some names have been changed
in order to protect privacy.

"Do consider planning for a Spring baby," enthused the Nurse. To a young woman eager to start a family, she made it sound appealingly simple. Instead, her words were to haunt me with their unconscious irony through the long years that followed. I think back fondly now to the days of my total naïvety. I set about the business of getting pregnant as if I could plan it and work at it precisely as I had set about everything else in my life. The first task on my mental list was to visit the Nurse at the local surgery for a chat about coming off the Pill. She advised waiting for at least three months before trying and maybe more if I wanted a bouncing Spring baby. Immediately the desire to do things correctly vied with my natural impatience.

"No way am I going to wait till the summer to get pregnant and have a Spring baby," I thought. "I want to be pregnant sooner than that. I want to be pregnant *now*."

I was in the perfect position to start a family. By February 1997, the month of my visit to the Nurse, I had been married to Jeremy for nearly three years and we had already achieved so many of our goals. Jeremy was offered a good job one week before our wedding. He finished his Engineering Ph.D. and we moved to Great Malvern for him to start work. At the time, I was in the second year of an English Ph.D. My research was practically complete and all that remained was to write it all up. We bought a semi, made one of the bedrooms into a study and I worked on my thesis there for the first year of our married life.

So there I was, well-educated, happily married, living in a beautiful place. It seemed to me so far that life had progressed in a very satisfying way. I had worked hard, been pretty sensible all along and reaped my rewards. I felt quite sure that God's plan for me was very nice indeed and I was glad to comply. Many of the harsh realities of life had passed me by and I happily assumed that they would continue to do so.

We both wanted to involve ourselves in the local community, keen to become part of Malvern life and to feel that we belonged. Everything else in life responded to a bit of planning, so we sat down and made a list. Firstly, I would find an evening dance class. Secondly, we would volunteer to help with a local Scout Troop. We met through the Scout and Guide Group at university and were eager to encourage Scouting experiences and values in local youngsters. Thirdly, we would find a Church (in that order, I'm afraid).

Again, it all progressed very well. I loved my dance class. The Scout District Commissioner assigned us to help restart a local Troop in a quiet area that had closed down for lack of leaders 18 months previously. We began to attend our nearest Church where the people were friendly and the style of service was modern and upbeat. We met a lot of people, began to make some friends and enjoyed taking on roles in which we felt needed.

At the end of 1995 I finished my Ph.D. thesis and was keen to find a job. Slightly perplexing, however, was the fact that I had no clear idea of what I wanted to do. I had an ambition to write but no specific inspiration to get me started. Sadly, no one would pay me to read works of literature all day! I worked voluntarily in the local Oxfam shop as my Ph.D. neared completion, so when paid part-time work became available in the clothes shop next door I decided to take it while I pondered what to do next.

Although I hoped not to be in the shop long-term, no experience is ever wasted and working there certainly opened my eyes to a world of lowly-paid employment. I started on far less than the minimum wage (which didn't exist when I began to work there) and although I was technically a part-time member of staff I found I was actually expected to be available for shifts at any time. I learned to get on with a wide spectrum of people. I learned how to calm angry customers. I also learned to do repetitive work conscientiously, keeping in mind that God was my true boss and could always see what I was up to!

On the positive side, I was no longer a student for the first time. I was in paid employment, with all sorts of possibilities ahead of me. I had developed feminist attitudes while at university and accordingly my priorities were career first and children second. I was determined that they would not be allowed to interfere with my right to a working life just as a man had. And then in late 1996, out of the blue, everything changed. Suddenly it was as if someone had flicked the switch that activated my maternal instincts. From that moment onwards, all my previous convictions, ambitions and desires were bowled over by a desperate urge to have a child. I was astonished and surprisingly powerless before it. Jeremy had always made it clear that he hoped to start a family before he turned 30 and I'd agreed to that without giving it much consideration. As a newly-married woman of 22, the grand old age of 30 seemed an awfully long way away. I had given little thought to children at all, feeling that I could put it off for years yet. But then maternal instincts hit and suddenly I couldn't cope with having to wait even a day. I wanted a baby and I wanted one NOW.

After the visit to the Nurse, I started taking vitamins, reading books about planning for a healthy baby and generally getting myself mentally prepared. In fact, preparing myself for a baby took over everything - what I ate, what I did, my every thought. Surely this was like everything else in life, I reasoned. If I turned my mind to it then I would reap my rewards just as usual.

I studiously ignored anything that might suggest otherwise. One of my new Church friends, Sally, was five years older than me and had had a long and painful experience of infertility, culminating in the news that she and her husband would never have children of their own. I listened to her and sympathised while remaining utterly convinced that such a thing could never happen to me. And yet, things went wrong from the very beginning. Going on the Pill a few years before had been difficult because several different types of pill had unpleasant side effects on me, but I did not realise that coming off it might also prove troublesome. At the surgery, the Nurse advised me to stop taking the Pill and wait for at least three months before we began trying to conceive. But swept away by my desire for a baby, I would suffer no delays. My plan was to wait for my first normal period and then start trying straight away. So I had a withdrawal bleed and then I waited, but I was totally confounded when my period never came. In fact, nothing happened for weeks and weeks. It was as if my body simply could not work out what had happened to it and what it should be doing. I was disappointed, but I knew that it had taken my Mum a whole 6 months to get pregnant with me, so I was well within that time limit.

After about three months of no period, I began to bleed a tiny bit every day and this continued for about 2 months. I put up with it for this long because I just could not figure out what was happening to me. Each day (and I thought about it continuously all day long) I pondered the same dilemmas. Was I already pregnant? Was this how my periods were going to be from now on? Was the strange bleeding going to stop today? Should I seek some help?

I would piece together in my mind all the signs and symptoms that could possibly indicate I was already pregnant and try to convince myself that I was. I even tried a couple of pregnancy tests, which, of course, were negative. I shook so much while waiting for the little blue line to appear and cried so hard when it showed that I wasn't pregnant that I resolved not to do another pregnancy test until I had much better evidence to go on. Meanwhile, life went on as usual. We worked, ran the Scout Troop and had a holiday in America visiting friends. The time crept past. Abandoning my feminist notions, I had stopped looking for another job because I was convinced that I would not be in the shop for much longer anyway. I would be pregnant and jolly and embarking on my new career of motherhood any day now. When we returned from our holiday in America and the strange bleeding still had not stopped, I finally realised I had to go and see the Doctor to discuss the non-appearance of normal periods. She prescribed some more hormone drugs to try to restart things.

I became very upset as my self-imposed 6-month time limit came and went. Continually creating false pressures was a very foolish thing to do. I looked at the example of other people (only the fertile ones) and assumed that I would be the same. The imagined deadlines came and went and only added to my stress and panic as time marched on with no pregnancy. I wish I had not tortured myself in that way. I know now that women have so many different experiences of menstruation, conception and pregnancy that it was useless and damaging to impose any expectations on myself at all. But I did not know that at the time. I thought everyone conceived easily and I would, too.

The hormone tablets made me have a 'normal' bleed and I was hopeful that my periods would then resume, but after a few weeks the bizarre bleeding began again. Reflecting on my experiences of the last six months and my previous difficulties with the Pill, I began to have an inkling that my body did not react quite as expected to hormone drugs. However, there didn't seem to be any alternative but to go back to the Doctor for more help. She gave me a second dose of the hormone drug. Again, it had no useful effect and I was left in a strange limbo. Finally, late in 1997 I started to menstruate normally. My periods had always been irregular and when they resumed they continued to be so. It had taken me more than ten months after coming off the Pill to have anything resembling a normal period. I felt I should have been half-way to having a baby by then, instead of which we were off to a very bad start. It was just my introduction to the unbelievable frustration and confusion of infertility.

However, at least we could get on with trying properly to conceive now. As anyone who has ever seriously set about the business of conceiving a baby will know, 'sex for babies' is different from sex for fun. Timing and location are more important than spontaneity and pleasure. Is it the right time of the month, before or during ovulation? Are we doing this somewhere that I can lay down afterwards with a pillow underneath me? Such were the pressures that began to invade what should have been a loving and pleasurable experience.

There were other pressures, too. I began to lead my life with a new mental attitude. I ate more healthily and tried to look after myself better, but I was also going further and acting as if I was already pregnant, just in case. I avoided all the foods a pregnant woman should avoid and gave up alcohol altogether. I worried about the affect of going to bed too late, heavy lifting or strenuous garden work. Because I did not know why I had so far failed to become pregnant I became more and more worried that something I was eating or doing could be the problem. Fortunately, in 1998, at the end of our first year of fertility problems, my very sensible Doctor talked things through with me and told me to stop eating and acting like a pregnant woman. She assured me that just going about my normal life and eating normal healthy food would not adversely affect my chances and that I should try to stop worrying so much. It was good advice and saved me from at least part of the pressure that was weighing me down.

There were, of course, psychological pressures that my Doctor could do nothing about. She could not clear all pregnant people from my path, for instance, or prevent me having to see people with sweet little children wherever I went. When we first began trying for a family of our own we knew very few people with young children. Of those who did have kids, the closest to us were Jeremy's older sister and her husband, who already had two before we even began to try.

Our niece and nephew had always been very important to us and they became even more precious as time went on. I was so grateful for the contact we had with them, learning a great deal about babies and young children from them. Most of all I learned that children abundantly reward the time and attention given them and I adored the relationship I had with them both.

The hardest thing of all was when our friends began to start families. I know it was very unreasonable of me to expect them to wait while we sorted our problems out, but it was unbelievably hard to hear their news when things were going so perplexingly wrong for us. As Jeremy gently pointed out to me once or twice, their pregnancies did not in any way affect us or our likelihood of success. Still, I always found their news hurtful, sometimes triggering an anguish so intense that it was actually a physical pain. I can only hope that I was good at concealing just how painful I found it. We hadn't yet told many people of our situation as I had barely begun to come to terms with it myself.

I vividly remember an important conversation with my close friend Laura. What she had to say was amazing. Before she even married, her Doctor told her that due to her almost non-existent periods she was more likely to win the lottery than to have a baby. Recently she had just reached a point in her spiritual life where she was on the verge of embracing the Christian faith and contemplating baptism. She had asked God in prayer to give her some confirmation of her decision. His answer to that prayer was the most wonderful and unexpected thing. Despite all her Doctor's confident predictions, she became pregnant. She even went on to be baptised while pregnant!

When she rang to tell me, I was so glad for her and amazed at what God had done. I kept smiling and chatting happily all the time the conversation lasted. But when I put the phone down the smile switched off, I took a deep shaky breath and I howled. Why her and not me? Why had *my* prayers not been answered, too? Did God not like me as much? Was my faith not strong enough? I had reached a point of deep frustration (I think this was while waiting for my periods even to begin normally), and I let it all out that night. I kicked the furniture, I threw cushions around and I screamed my anger and frustration aloud. I should have been delighted for her as a friend and a new Christian, and on one level I was, but I was so taken over by my own situation that I could hardly see beyond it. If this makes me sound very mean, impatient and self-obsessed, it's because that's exactly how I was.

As time went on, I found it harder and harder to be with pregnant people, although it seemed to become easier once the babies were born because I still enjoyed being around children. But pregnancy was the gateway to having children and it was pregnancy that I hated to see because for some unknown reason it was denied to me. Pregnant women were all around me and my thoughts circled in the same unhelpful loops. Why can teenage girls with no desire for a child catch by accident, but I, who want one desperately, cannot? I had apparently done everything right by God's standards - found just the right man, married him, worked hard, set up home and then, with all this love, stability and cosiness to offer, gone ahead and tried to conceive. How come everyone else in the world could have babies and I couldn't? I was just beginning to grasp that very often the hand that we are dealt in life is *not* fair, and that we are not always going to see rewards for the things that we do. The world is full of suffering and pain. But beginning to acknowledge this, and that it affected me as much as every other human being, just made me feel even more helpless.

Perhaps I would never have a baby. I couldn't face that idea. But if the waiting and speculating involved in a single month of trying could seem to go on forever, how could I endure years of trying? I knew then that I couldn't endure, and that I would become appallingly desperate and embittered. Worst of all, my prayers at that time were always the same. Never, Your will be done, Lord, or please help me to endure, but instead, Lord, please give me a baby this month, please give me a baby now, I can't wait, please don't make me wait a moment longer.

2

There were harder experiences yet to come before we received any glimmer of hope. One of them was my visit to a maternity unit with my friend Laura. We happened to go and stay with her towards the end of her miraculous pregnancy and she had an appointment for a scan. She invited me to go along and I agreed, curious to see what the scan was like, but without any real awareness of what was involved. I soon found out. We had to sit and wait for nearly an hour in a room full of heavily pregnant women. Everywhere I turned, my eyes rested on a pregnant form. They all sat there, hands resting on distended stomachs, grumbling about being pregnant, discussing whether they were on their first, third, sometimes fourth pregnancy.

My attention ricocheted between listening to them and the demands of my own anguished internal monologue. I began to feel increasingly hysterical. After a while I couldn't stand it any more. I hid in the loos for a few minutes sobbing hard, dry sobs and wondering how to escape. I tried to calm down and I prayed, please Lord, help me through this. And then I took a deep breath, went back out and rejoined Laura. Part of me was glad that I did because I had the privilege of seeing the scanned images of Laura's unborn baby, which were amazing. But mostly I think I should have been far more sensible. I should have declined to accompany her and waited with Jeremy who was hanging around in a nearby secondhand bookshop.

Afterwards, we joined Jeremy in the bookshop. I felt unspeakably weary and miserable, but books usually have a cheering effect on me. Ever since the beginning of my Ph.D. I had been searching for anything by Charlotte Smith, the eighteenth century author I wrote my thesis on, in every secondhand bookshop I passed. I had trawled through thousands of books with no success, but that day when I glumly set about my usual search, there was something rather special waiting for me on a nice prominent shelf – a fifth edition of Charlotte Smith's *Elegiac Sonnets* in beautiful condition, dated 1789. And it was affordable. I couldn't believe my eyes. Of course, I bought it straight away and showed it off proudly to Laura and her husband later. They must have thought I was mad to get so excited about a musty old book, but it was an excellent distraction for me and raised my spirits. Never before or since have I stumbled across anything by that author despite years of searching. It just so happens that it turned up when I had been through an extremely difficult afternoon. More importantly, an afternoon on which I had remembered to ask for God's help.

Later in 1998 we heard from my sister-in-law that she was expecting her third baby. Again I found the news very difficult to take. I could hardly bare to look at her pregnant stomach or endure a conversation about the new baby. I stopped seeking out her company because hiding from it as much as possible was the only way I could cope with the physical fact of the pregnancy, although we still saw them for family occasions like birthdays and Christmas. I felt so bitter, frustrated and desperate.

By this point, I had been having periods again for months, but still I failed to become pregnant. My Doctor referred me to a Gynaecologist at the Royal Infirmary in Worcester and I waited for my appointment, slightly happier knowing that we would soon receive some expert help. The Gynaecologist reviewed what the Doctor had to say about my strange experiences coming off the pill and my irregular periods and decided that the thing to do was to make sure I was ovulating, so he prescribed Clomiphene (Clomid). I was alarmed at the idea of more false hormones, but for the most part very relieved that someone had listened to me and was trying to help. I was also referred for a Hysterosalpingogram and Jeremy was scheduled for a sperm test.

In the meantime I tried to distract myself. Work occupied too little of my mental energy so I threw myself into Scouts, investing a great deal of time, energy and emotion into working for the Troop. It was extremely rewarding, but not enough. By the late autumn of 1998, I was deep in the doldrums. I can remember sitting alone in the house one gloomy afternoon feeling utterly bleak, seeing nothing but darkness around me. A crisis was looming. Ever expecting my new life of parenthood to begin, I had allowed myself to put everything else on hold for too long, particularly the search for a new job, but my negative mood affected this, too. Just as it seemed impossible to conceive, so I felt it was impossible for me to escape my job. I had lost all sense of the real me and I was sinking into despair. It was a horrid sensation.

Then some of our university friends came to visit for a weekend and their interesting conversation and encouragement suddenly reminded me that I could take control of my working life if I wanted to. I remember conversing with them and feeling astonished that it was me speaking so intelligently! That weekend I began to think seriously about looking for another job regardless of the baby situation. It was then that I realised that for a long time I had forgotten to pray about anything other than babies. It had not occurred to me to ask God to help me out of the hole I was in, in a way other than a pregnancy. So I turned to Him in my time of crisis and also asked my Church Housegroup to pray. Within two weeks I had begun a new job! I was puzzled that God answered the prayer about a job so quickly yet not the hundreds of prayers I had uttered about a baby, but I was deeply grateful to have a new focus. The start of the New Year (1999) saw a more optimistic me.

My working life as an Administrator for a small company suited me much better. I found the work enjoyably challenging and I embarked on the job with two new attitudes. The first was that I was going to be absolutely open about my faith and even try to be a good witness to my colleagues. Buoyed up by the immediate answer to my desperate request for a job, I stated my faith clearly on my CV. It nearly lost me the job. My boss told me later that my colleagues had been very doubtful about whether a Christian would be a comfortable person to have around. Would I sport a righteous frown and spontaneously combust if someone swore? However, they decided to give me a chance and I saw it as an opportunity to prove to them that Christian does not equal weirdo! My office was about one and a half miles up the hill from home so I walked there every morning praying on the way. At lunchtime I walked home again back down the hill. I loved it, and I have no doubt that I was better able to face the challenges of my new job because of all the prayer. In fact, it was a really good time, as I became much more physically and spiritually fit!

My second new attitude was that of greater self-respect. At the shop I had allowed myself to be treated as a doormat, accepting extremely low pay and random hours and often having to drop all my own plans when called in to work at the last minute. At the new company I was determined to stand up for myself more. I was contracted to work part-time and I decided that this meant that the rest of my time belonged to me. For a person who loathes any kind of confrontation or disagreement I knew that this would be a very hard thing to do but I also knew that I had to start as I meant to go along. I prayed about it and when the opportunity arose I took it. The first time my boss asked me if I could stay on into the afternoon I had already made plans to work on Scout admin at home. Also, I had no lunch with me and when you are on a low wage, having to buy your own lunch really eats into your pay. So I very politely but firmly said no, I could not stay that day but perhaps I would another time with a little more notice. And then I left as usual. I shook most of the way home and wondered if I would get the sack. But for the rest of our working relationship my employer treated me with the utmost respect and understanding and I believe that that moment of assertiveness early on truly helped.

So in the end Christmas 1998 was busy and happy. My excitement over my new job, fundraising for a new roof for the Scout hut and the fact that three of our Scouts had managed to achieve their Chief Scout's Award lifted me out of my gloom and gave me other more joyful things to focus on. My desire for a baby didn't go on the backburner for long, but I did feel calmer about it.

Meanwhile, I was still working my way through the prescription of Clomid and occasionally having experiences which alarmed and puzzled me. Several times in the night I was woken by an absolutely agonising pain in my abdomen that lasted for about 15 minutes. Much later I came to the conclusion that the extra stimulus of the Clomid had caused a painful reaction in my ovaries. At the time, however, it left me feeling shaky and depressed. A few days after the last painful episode, I was reading my way through the book of Psalms and praying, 'please let me read something hopeful about children, please give me a hopeful message.' A moment later I came to Psalms 127 and 128, which suddenly filled me with hope.

Psalm 127

> If the Lord does not build the house, the work of the builders is useless;
> If the Lord does not protect the city it is useless for the sentries to stand guard.

It is useless to work so hard for a living, getting up early and going to bed late.
For the Lord provides for those he loves, while they are asleep.

Children are a gift from the Lord;
they are a real blessing.
The sons a man has when he is young are like arrows in a soldier's hand.
Happy is the man who has many such arrows.
He will never be defeated when he meets his enemies in the place of judgement.

Psalm 128

Happy are those who obey the Lord, who live by his commands.

Your work will provide for your needs;
You will be happy and prosperous.
Your wife will be like a fruitful vine in your home, and your sons will be like young olive-trees round your table.
A man who obeys the Lord will surely be blessed like this.

May the Lord bless you from Zion!
May you see Jerusalem prosper all the days of your life!
May you live to see your grandchildren!

Peace be with Israel!

Good News Bible

It's pretty obvious which bits of those wonderful Psalms appealed to me the most. In particular, the image of 'sons around your table' stuck in my mind ever after that day. I wondered if I could take it as a promise to me from God that one day I would be surrounded by my children, coming as it did so promptly after my fervent and heartfelt prayer for a hopeful message. I was heartened by what I had read and I resumed prayer for a baby, wondering if God really did have children in mind for me. However, the part of the Psalms that failed to register was the strong theme of obedience to God's plans and commands. I still did not ask what He wanted me to do. My prayers were still *my* will be done, not Yours. I wrote in my diary:

25ᵗʰ ***February, 1999*** *I'm so disappointed. My period has just arrived when I was so hopeful. I was on day 39 of my cycle and it normally lasts about 36 days, so my hopes were rising. Now they're at an end yet again. Discovered a few days ago that a friend from Church, Helen, had an ectopic pregnancy 6 years ago which ended at 11 weeks and she has been trying unsuccessfully to get pregnant ever since. She's 33 now. She described the end of a cycle as a 'monthly bereavement' and that's so true. It's the death of the baby you could have had, and also of another month's worth of hope. I'm going to pray every day that she conceives, as well as for me. How unbearable to go through it for 6 years. I hope and pray fervently that this isn't the case for me.*

Another thing I hadn't yet recognised was that I was gently being led into a small community of Christian women who had also suffered the pain of infertility. Although I still tried hard to believe that I was not the same as them, they did give me immense comfort as I struggled through the early years of infertility. A few months later I had another hard experience to go through, but my diary shows that I was turning more and more to God for the strength and fortitude that I did not have myself and that He gave them to me when I asked.

1ˢᵗ ***April, 1999*** *I haven't written for nearly a month, but I'm on holiday for a week and a half now, so maybe I'll have a chance to catch up. The main news is that we have a new niece! I have been praying hard that I'm not afflicted by jealousy and having seen her today I'm glad to say that I was only happy and pleased with her and not jealous at all.*

13ᵗʰ ***April, 1999*** *... today I thoroughly enjoyed playing with my niece and nephew and cuddling the new baby. What gorgeous children! I'm so glad I prayed for help combatting my bitterness and jealousy, because I found myself able simply to enjoy their society. I bathed them and read them stories till they fell asleep. My nephew came out with a classic line, which, at the age of 3, I thought was hilarious. The baby was crying upstairs and I asked him what he thought she was saying. He piped up instantly, "She's saying I want a bath in the cat litter," which had us all in stitches!*

Meanwhile our own saga rolled slowly on. My appointment for a Hysterosalpingogram came through and I trundled off to the Worcester Royal Infirmary. I knew that this was a test to check that my fallopian tubes had no obvious problems or blockages and that it would be a bit uncomfortable. I had to go to the Royal Infirmary and as with many other appointments, I went alone. Jeremy or Mum would willingly have come with me but I didn't like to make a drama out of nothing and I was absolutely ignorant about how each new treatment or test would affect me until afterwards. With hindsight, I now wish that Jeremy had accompanied me to more of the early appointments and tests because I often found myself more distressed afterwards than I thought I would be and I was, after all, going through it for both our sakes.

Anyway, alone at the hospital, I was sent to a small cubicle to change into a gown. Then a female Nurse led me into a room and I was asked to lay on a table with a sheet covering my lower half. The Nurse was present. The Doctor used a metal instrument to squirt ink into my fallopian tubes. I was then scanned and the Doctor turned the screen around so that I could see a new view of myself - my reproductive system with the progress of the ink along my tubes highlighted in a darker colour. It was uncomfortable and gave me an ache like period pain, but was quite interesting on the whole.

The Doctor pronounced my tubes all clear and I felt relieved and frustrated all over again. It was good to discover that there was nothing to prevent eggs travelling down my fallopian tubes if I ovulated (although that was, of course, still in question), but on the other hand, we were no closer to explaining our lack of success in conceiving. I was allowed to go back into the cubicle to change and it was then that I found myself leaning on the wall with tears streaming down my face. The test had been uncomfortable and undignified, that was part of it, but the main reason for my tears and sudden self-pity was because this was not how the conception of our child was supposed to be. I wanted our baby to result from a moment of intimacy and love, not from cold rooms and metal instruments and waiting lists for the next set of tests. Why did this have to happen to us? I wished with my whole heart that everything was quite different.

Jeremy had to have his test, too. His sperm test came back with an encouraging result. He had an immensely high sperm count and although a low level of motility was also detected (in other words, lots of the sperm cells were stationary instead of swimming hard as an active sperm should) the Doctor felt that the low motility was offset by the good count. I was relieved again, although this clearly left the finger of blame pointing at me. I had to come to terms with the feelings of guilt that came with that notion and also increased frustration that we still had absolutely no idea what was going wrong.

Meanwhile, I was still working my way through my batch of Clomid, but as usual things failed to go smoothly and it took me some months to work out what was happening. The Clomid worked, it did make me ovulate. I had become quite an expert by this point in interpreting the signs displayed by my body because I hardly thought about anything else all day long, so I could feel that it was working. But because my cycles remained long and rather irregular the monthly blood test I had to have at the Surgery to establish whether I was ovulating or not always came back negative. I was always tested as if the middle of my cycle was around Day 14, as it is for most women. My middle or ovulation point was actually about Day 20, as my cycles were between 33-36 days long, but none of the medical staff ever took this into account. I was in confusion again, torn between the evidence of my own body and my desire to believe that the medical professionals always knew best.

After 6 months of Clomid and no pregnancy, I returned to the Gynaecologist in Worcester to give a progress report. This time, I was shown in to see a Registrar who I'd never seen before. He glanced at my notes briefly before deciding that as the blood tests clearly showed that I wasn't ovulating, the dose of Clomid should be doubled. I felt very uneasy about this but was too inexpert and too used to doing what I was told to refuse. I went home and took the first double dose.

18th May, 1999 So I'm 28! I wouldn't mind at all, except that it makes me a little anxious to find myself 28 and still childless. If one's fertility decreases with age, won't a family become less likely? I'm feeling a bit low (PMT), hence this negativity. Also, since the Gynaecologist doubled my dose of Clomid, my cycle has lasted 48 days so far and I'm still counting. Surely this is not helpful?

It was not. The higher dose had the bizarre effect of causing me to have a cycle of 76 days in length, with a very uncomfortable ovulation fifteen days before the end of it. Obviously, this was completely missed by the Day 14 blood test and it was at this point that I rebelled and decided that I would never again take any more fake hormones. I had had enough of being tampered with by Doctors who obviously didn't understand as much about my body as I did. I had had enough of hormone drugs and their weird effects. I had put my hope and trust in the drugs and the Doctors for several years with not even a hint of a pregnancy to show for it. According to my medical records it looked as if the problem was my non-ovulation, which I knew to be untrue.

I stormed back to my Doctor refusing to take any more Clomid (which she agreed with) and asked to be referred back to the Gynaecologist once more with the intention of explaining to him exactly what effect his hormone drugs had on me. I wanted to insist that I *was* ovulating, so our problem must be something else. What's more, I asked the Doctor to ensure that I saw the Consultant Gynaecologist himself this time as I was in no state to see yet another unknown medic who was utterly unacquainted with my case. My Doctor was very good and agreed to write a letter to the Consultant that ensured I would see him in person. As I wrote in my diary:

24th May, 1999 I saw my doctor last Wednesday and she agreed with everything I said, so I'm having a rest from the Clomid but the blood tests will continue. My friend Caroline suggested taking Oil of Evening Primrose which is supposed to be helpful at regulating hormones, so I bought some straight away. It's such a relief not to be on the drugs anymore. Oh please let me get pregnant naturally, Father.

As this entry shows, my sudden lack of faith in modern medicine began to take the direction of searching for alternative forms of help. I was desperate for a natural conception after all the unpleasant experiences of the last few years and I also longed for proof that I was ovulating naturally to confirm my own conclusions.

It helped that by then I was able to be quite open with my close friends about our problems. I have always found talking things through very beneficial and God had sent me good friends through the Church who I turned to more and more, especially Sally who was about five years ahead of me in her own infertility saga. She was very helpful in listening to my woes and telling me about how she had begun to come to terms with her own situation, despite still being upset about it. I remember respecting her enormously for her acceptance of the situation and can also remember my other reaction – surely this will not happen to us. Please let us not really be infertile. Please let us not have to accept life without children. If we did remain childless, I was utterly convinced that I could never learn to accept the situation as Sally had done.

3

A couple of months passed while we waited for the appointment with the Consultant Gynaecologist. I desperately needed to see someone with the authority to reassure me after my recent experiences. I was certainly in no psychological state to cope with another Doctor that I'd never met before, who had had all of two minutes to review my case, and who might make a decision about me that could send my body haywire again. My own Doctor had promised that I would see the Consultant himself and I was greatly relieved. I can remember saying to my Mum after discussing the double-dose-of-Clomid disaster, "but it's ok because this time I'm seeing the big man himself." I was tense and stressed about the whole situation again and I just could not fathom why my body did not appear to work like everyone else's.

When it was time to see the Consultant, I was sensible and asked Jeremy to accompany me. I felt I needed moral support to enable me to stand up for myself, especially if I felt unhappy with the suggestions made by the Consultant or if I was offered another set of drugs that I didn't want to take. We sat in the corridor rather tensely for half an hour or so and then my name was called. We filed into a small consulting room only to be greeted by a young woman Registrar who I'd never seen before. It was more than I could stand. I can't remember whether I actually burst into tears or not, but I was certainly on the verge of howling as I stammered out,

"My Doctor promised I would see the Consultant himself. Please, I need to see the actual Consultant." The young woman was a bit nonplussed, but she kindly agreed to go and see if it would be possible for me to see him.

Jeremy and I waited in tense silence in her room. I was trying to cope with the disappointment of what had just happened as well as the agitating after-shock of having asserted myself. When she returned, she informed us that we would be able to see the Consultant but that we would have to wait for a while longer, probably an hour or so. I readily agreed and we escaped back to the waiting area. I felt as exhausted as if I had done battle. When I was calm again Jeremy proposed that he should take a quick trip to the nearby shops to buy a birthday card for a friend. I agreed as we still had 45 minutes to wait. About five minutes after he'd gone, my name was called and I realised with a sinking heart that I would have to face the much-awaited appointment alone after all. I went in and sat down opposite the Consultant who was studying my notes. This is how I described what happened in my diary:

17th June, 1999 Bad news again, I'm afraid. We nearly ended up seeing yet another Registrar but I kicked up a fuss and insisted on seeing the expert. It was worth it - he cut through all the pfaffing about with drugs in a moment, but what he said was such a shock. Basically, according to all tests there's nothing obviously wrong but we have been trying for 2½ years without a hint of a pregnancy. Therefore, we fall into the 'sub-fertile' category. Therefore, there is no point dabbling with drugs, our main chance is with an assisted pregnancy. So we can go on the waiting list for IVF treatment. This shocked me through and through, although I am grateful for his plain dealing. IVF is so unnatural, so drastic. I suppose the thing that is hardest of all is that we now have to accept that we are infertile.

The Consultant went on to offer me two options, either a referral to the Women's Hospital (NHS) or the Priory Hospital (private), both in Birmingham. He advised me to get my name down quickly for the Women's Hospital, if that was my choice, as the waiting list was rather long.

17th June, 1999 (cont.) This area has very little funding for fertility treatment and it could be years - at least 2 or 3 - before our names are at the top. We could go privately, but it would cost around £1400 each time. Apparently the success rate is still fairly low.

And that was it. I was so shocked I could not think of a single question to ask, so I thanked him politely and left. I walked out of the hospital in a daze, my thoughts whirling, trying rather confusedly to find Jeremy. I set off quickly around the outside of the hospital heading for a quiet road that led to the city centre and ran straight into him returning hastily. I buried my head in his jacket and wailed, "He's referring us for IVF, there's nothing else they can do," and then burst into tears.

We stood together in the middle of the street while I sobbed my heart out. Then I told Jeremy exactly what had happened and we walked quietly back to the car, holding onto each other, shell-shocked and watching our dream of a family disappear even further into the distance.

We managed to discuss the unexpected turn of events calmly and reasonably later on that day. I wrote:

*17ᵗʰ **June, 1999** (cont.) So we have a decision before us. How long are we prepared to keep trying unassisted before feeling that it's time to get this kind of help? Jeremy said he has no problem with paying for the treatment. How long, then? And should we also look into adoption while we have time in hand to put ourselves on a waiting list? What I hope and pray for is that we will conceive naturally now that my body isn't being disrupted by drugs. If only we could see the future and know which decisions to make. I feel a bit better knowing that God can see it all, the little sagas of our unimportant lives, and hopefully He'll guide us. What kind parents I have. A while ago I phoned Mum with today's news (inevitably bursting into tears on her) and she said that if we want private IVF treatment, we mustn't worry about the money. But the psychological trauma is the real stumbling block.*

I summed things up sensibly that day, but my real feelings were more complicated and took longer for me to explore. Now that 'unexplained infertility' was our official diagnosis, I had to accept that we were really and truly an infertile couple. That was hard enough. But I was still so anxious over the affects my recent experiences of hormone drugs had had on me, that I was horrified by the idea of an even more unnatural process like IVF. And then there was the faith side of things. Surely something as drastic and unnatural as IVF could never be part of God's plan for us. My God, I thought, can certainly give me a baby naturally – look at Sarah, or Hannah, or Elizabeth in the Bible - so surely all I need is more faith, more prayers and more patience. Typically, Jeremy proposed a sensible course of action, suggesting we just think about it for a while and perhaps look into IVF before we made any decisions.

I wish I had been offered counselling at this point, but we weren't even given as much as an informative leaflet to assist us in our decision. While struggling to cope with my grief over our inability to produce a child and my distress at our new label of 'unexplained infertility', the only fact about IVF I could conjure to mind was the news about the first test tube baby I had heard when I was about 10 years old. Then, as now at 28, it all sounded very weird, and nothing whatever to do with me.

My strongest emotions won out in the end. Based on my accumulated experiences of the affect of fake hormones, all my feelings were utterly against any consideration of IVF. I did not want to know anything more about it because I could not face the idea of my children being conceived in a test tube. It wasn't just a tarnishment of my dream of becoming a mother, like the other tests had been, it was the complete obliteration of that dream. As far as I could see it was the end of all naturalness, normality, romance and any other good thing that I had ever imagined about conceiving a child. My heart, my mind and my soul all said 'No!' and 'No!' is what they continued to say over the following weeks. IVF was the total antithesis of everything I had hoped and prepared myself for since we first began to try for a baby years before.

When I told Jeremy how I felt he was so understanding. He suggested that we should just wait till I felt ready to consider the dreaded subject further and in the meantime keep trying. We agreed to a time limit of roughly 18 months, during which I felt hopeful that perhaps I would become pregnant naturally. After all, our diagnosis of 'unexplained infertility' didn't really tell us anything. We knew a lot by then of what *wasn't* wrong with us, but we still didn't know what the real problem was, so as far as we could see there was still a chance of a natural pregnancy. I had just turned 28 and although we'd already been trying for several years by this point, at least we had started fairly young, so it felt as if time was on our side. If we still hadn't conceived at the end of the 18 months, we would discuss the more drastic approach of IVF, but not just now.

When the Consultant wrote to enquire whether I had made up my mind about which hospital I would like to be referred to I wrote back stating that we were not ready for IVF treatment and preferred him to hold off on his referral for the time being. And that was the end of the issue, I felt. Surely in the long 18 months ahead I would become pregnant and this difficult story would have a happy conclusion, the happy conclusion that *I* had in mind. It still did not occur to me that God might have other plans for me, so I stubbornly persisted in doing things my way without ever stopping to ask.

I was sure that there had to be a better, more natural, way to achieve a pregnancy, so I began to pour my thoughts and energies into this alternative route. My periods were still not back to normal after the Clomid disaster. I became obsessed by the stages of my monthly cycle, even more so than before because I was desperate for things to go back to normal quickly. I carefully tracked the end of my period, the run-up to ovulation, the sensations of ovulation, then the inevitable 'sex for babies', followed by the point at which my hormones would change and PMT struck, and those last awful days before my period started again when I tried desperately to convince myself that I must, must surely, be pregnant this time.

I returned with vigour to a full consideration of everything that we did and ate. But it was no longer enough that I had given up all alcohol, ate mainly organic, healthy food, and took pregnancy vitamins, or that I had foisted a lot of this on Jeremy, too (not the pregnancy vitamins, obviously!). I needed more, I needed help of some kind, a plan or programme so I could feel that we were moving closer to our goal all the time. The alternative was black despair, as month after month another chance came and went.

When we first planned to start a family several years before I avidly read a book called *Planning for a Healthy Baby*, loaned to me by a family friend. It was from that book that I had gleaned the advice about a healthy diet and lifestyle which had informed the basis of my thinking for the last few years. I suddenly remembered that the book had mentioned an organisation called Foresight which helped people to try alternative methods to achieve a natural pregnancy. I was afraid it might turn out to be costly, but I took the plunge and contacted them anyway because I was so desperate for someone to offer me the kind of help that I could cope with. They agreed to treat me as a postal patient and Jeremy and I both had to send off hair samples for analysis to see if we were obviously deficient in vitamins or minerals that were vital for our reproductive health. We also had to fill in questionnaires about our general health, diet and lifestyle and our previous history of infertility. It all took some time, but improved my mood because we were doing something. I often spoke to the Practice Manager on the phone and she was kind and reassuring, pointing out that even if the vitamins and minerals didn't work, at least we would be as healthy as possible if we did have to embark on IVF.

Then I had the news from my close friend Caroline that she was pregnant. She and her husband had just returned from a posting in America and the time was right for them to start their family. Most of my other friends who had shared this news with me over the years lived some distance away, but Caroline was a local friend from Church. I found it terribly hard to cope with, not only because it came just a few weeks after our final distressing visit to the Consultant, but also because in the past we had happily planned to have our children together. Caroline knew that we were having problems and this made breaking the news to me very difficult for her, too. She invited me round for coffee and then told me her news as gently as she could and her eyes were shiny with tears. I managed to smile and show some delight for her and I didn't cry until I was back at home by myself. Engulfed by the usual anguish, I also felt a sense of desolation because Caroline was going forward on the adventure of motherhood without me, and I didn't know if I would ever follow her. But the thing that hurt most of all was that when Caroline told me her wonderful news, she was crying out of sympathy for me instead of laughing with joy for herself. I felt desperately guilty for marring her special moment.

In the midst of all this, God had not forgotten us. Yet again at a dark time, I had a positive encounter with His love that lifted my spirits when they were at their lowest. One weekend, we were invited to stay with some friends for their housewarming party. They had moved to a lovely village and their house was opposite the beautiful old parish Church, so we went to the service there the next morning. There were only a dozen people there, but they had a new Vicar keen to reinvigorate the Church. I wondered where she saw her ministry focussing and in the course of the service she made it clear that her aim was to instigate a healing ministry. I thought that was wonderful and was even more interested when she said that during Communion, anyone who wished could go to the side of the Church to be prayed for by a team of 3 women. Jeremy grabbed my hand at that point and I knew what he wanted us to do, so after we'd taken Communion we went over and asked that they would pray for us to have children. It was a lovely feeling, sitting in a sunlit corner of the Church with kindly hands laid upon us, holding each other's hands while the ladies prayed for us. It was all very discreetly done and our friend also went for prayer which meant that we didn't feel awkward. Afterwards we departed for home and I felt amazingly uplifted and hopeful and excited. We stopped at Clumber Park for lunch and had a walk in the grounds and talked it all over. Jeremy said he felt that God was trying to meet us halfway and I shared how grateful I felt that we'd been given an opportunity to receive prayer like that because increasingly I had been feeling an urge to ask people for prayer.

A few days later, we went to assist some friends from Church who were about to move away from Malvern. While the men loaded the van, I sat with Barbara and we talked and then prayed together. She told me that she had to wait 6 years for her first child, so she understood exactly how I felt. She prayed in tongues over me, which I'd never heard before and it was a thrilling experience. We prayed about three times and again I felt so hopeful and excited. Also, she gently suggested that I might need to ask forgiveness for some of my previous selfish thinking, such as placing my rights as a woman way above the well-being of any children I might have. In my very feminist phase I was determined to have my way regardless of anyone else. Now I could see clearly that I had used feminism as an excuse for utter selfishness. I asked God to forgive me and from that day onwards began to be far more egalitarian in my thinking.

Barbara's suggestion of the need for forgiveness came as quite a revelation to me. It had never occurred to me before that my attitudes and actions from the time *before* I really began to seek for God, from the time before I knew what His standards were, could still count against me. I had a sort of idea that if I did something wrong but didn't know at the time that it was wrong, it didn't really count. And so I tried to dismiss all past wrongdoing from my mind. But that day I suddenly realised that God knew about it even if I didn't acknowledge His existence or standards at the time and that they were still offences against Him. I also realised that He wanted me to recognise these sins, admit that I was wrong and ask His forgiveness because He was desperately eager to wipe all the bad things away so that there wouldn't be any barriers between us. Wow! Alone later on I found myself in floods of tears admitting wrongdoing and knowing that at last I could genuinely put those bits of the past behind me.

In other areas of life I kept myself extremely busy as usual in order to distract my mind from the underlying trauma of infertility. We had friends and family to visit, went on holiday to Germany and ran another lovely Scout Camp. The summer passed quickly but I began to feel down again as winter approached, particularly because my periods were still very erratic after coming off Clomid months before.

23rd **November, 1999** *I've been very down for a few weeks, because just when I thought my 'monthly' cycle was settling down, things seem to have gone* *haywire and I don't know what's happening to me. My last cycle was down to a respectable 32 days, but this month 32 came and went. It is now 43 days since my last period began with no sign of the next one starting. Yes, I know it sounds as if I must be pregnant, and believe me I have been as high as a kite for days thinking my chance has come at last, but I have done two pregnancy tests (on day 37 and today) and both showed that I am not pregnant. So what is going on? After each test my mood has plummeted as low as it previously was high and I have found the impinging despair hard to cope with. My biggest fear now is that everything has stopped working again like when I came off the Pill, but this time I feel I can't go to the Doctor, because she just flings drugs at the problem and I think it's pretty obvious that they haven't helped. The degree of anguish caused by this situation is greater than any I have ever felt. I am also terrified that Jess, a work colleague, will become pregnant soon, as she has confessed to me that she and her husband want to start a family (she knows nothing of my troubles). I know I cannot cope with a pregnant woman at work every day. I can hardly cope with Caroline's pregnancy and I only see her once a week. Can God hear my prayers at all?*

*1ˢᵗ **December, 1999** … about 10 minutes after I finished writing my last entry, my period started. I felt very relieved, but the next day I couldn't stop crying. I just cried and cried, and prayed and pleaded and railed. I don't know how much more I can take. The despair is unbearable and even today, a week later, all I can see is despair behind me and despair laying wait in front. Underlying everything now, my every thought, is the fear of falling into that emptiness again and again in the coming months and years. I feel as if all real hope of having a child has been sucked out of me, as well as any clear idea of where I'm headed. Help, oh please help me to see a way forward. I don't know what I want or who I am, except that I have a need for a child which I can do nothing about.*

I was very angry with God for His total silence on the subject of our infertility at this point. But despite my doubts, He did hear my prayers and proof of it came shortly afterwards. One day at work I walked past my colleague Jess and a very clear voice said to me, "she's pregnant." It was inside my head and sounded like my voice, except that it was much more authoritative. I spent the rest of the day silently pondering the news. I knew it was the truth and I wondered if it was God speaking to me. When, some weeks later, Jess actually announced to us all that she was pregnant, I mentioned to her that I had known it since that particular day weeks ago. She was very surprised and replied,

"But that was before I knew it myself!"

I didn't explain to her how I knew, just treasured it up, thought about it and thanked God from the bottom of my heart. Because I had been given that knowledge before everyone else, even Jess herself, I had had a chance to accept the idea, I hadn't had to have my first exposure to her news in front of all my colleagues and I had been helped to do what I had declared impossible – I *had* coped, and continued to cope, with the fact of a pregnant woman at work every day, drawing strength from God's intervention. He did care about me after all.

Worrying about my strange cycles, I decided I needed some reassurance that things were still working. I had heard about a form of natural contraception called Persona, where you urinate on little sticks which react to your level of hormones and then slot them into a monitor for it to read and plot what is happening in your body. Obviously the intention of the system was to flag up when you were ovulating so that you could avoid unprotected sex at that point of the month in order to prevent a pregnancy. I bought the kit with the opposite intention and was really delighted and encouraged by the results.

18ʰ December, 1999 ... this month I started using Persona and lo and behold, on Day 17, a little 'o' for ovulation appeared! I was really pleased. So I do ovulate on my own at a reasonable point in my cycle. That's what the drugs were supposed to make me do and I don't need them. So we do have a chance of conceiving. Thank God! (I did).

After my severely bleak patch in November and early December, things were looking up again and I was praying more for the Lord's help.

24ʰ December, 1999 I want to thank God for His help in coping with the news that Laura is pregnant again. I managed to feel surprisingly glad for her. Our Foresight stuff arrived on Tuesday, informing us that we both have a Zinc deficiency, Jeremy has a Chromium deficiency, and I must make sure to eat often and sensibly as an imbalance in blood sugar level affects female hormones. It recommended a programme of vitamins and minerals for 3 months, which we'll try in the New Year. Please God, let it work.

My spirits rose again as we embarked on a new plan of treatment and also in response to another significant experience. On Boxing Day we took my Grampy to Church so that he could share in the Communion for the second time in his life. The previous time was 73 years earlier at his Confirmation! I came away with a strong sense that I needed to work on humility because the word kept hitting me like a hammer throughout the service. I suddenly realised I needed some true humility, like Jesus had, who was the first in the world but willingly put Himself last. I returned from Church that day and slipped upstairs, where I lay face down on the floor and asked God to forgive me for always putting myself and my own wishes first and rarely considering anyone else's and, in particular, for *never* considering that God Himself might have a plan for me. This was the first time that I began to wonder what that plan could be and whether having children was in it at all. In the New Year, I wrote:

26th January, 2000 On New Year's Eve, we enjoyed a great Millenium party with Church friends. I have no profound observations to make on the end of the 1990s and the beginning of the 2000s. Nothing portentous happened, even the 'millenium bug' was a damp squib. All I can say is that for me one year ended and the next began in excellent company and in a place that I love. We thought of each other and of God, and if one night can possibly set the stage for a whole year, then I have no complaints of that beginning.

So far this year God has given me a very great gift indeed and that is a little of the humility that I prayed for at Christmas. It has been so hard to submit to His will over the child issue, but I can finally say 'Your will be done' and really mean it. It isn't the right time for us yet but I can now rely on God choosing the best time and I know that there is no point in worrying and working myself up. It's not resignation that I feel but peace and a burden lifted from me. In His time is fine by me now. It's so much easier when we're pulling the same way.

4

My parents had been trying to sell their cottage in Buckinghamshire for some time and had finally found a buyer. They also found somewhere to move to, so their sale was slowly proceeding in the way that these things do, when the whole project came to a disappointing end. The sale fell through, the cottage had to go on the market again and they were back to square one. However, I was suddenly bitten by the moving bug and began seriously to think about whether it was time for us to make a move from our little semi into something a bit bigger. Persuading Jeremy was the most difficult bit as he is very averse to change and upheaval.

Early in the New Year, Jeremy agreed that we could start looking at houses to see if we could afford something worth moving to. As with the new job, it did me a great deal of good to concentrate on another area of our lives. Very quickly we found what we wanted, a much bigger house in a slightly neglected state that we could just about afford. We made an offer, it was accepted and we moved in at the beginning of April 2000. I remember our first night in the new house, sitting in bed at 5.30 a.m. unable to sleep because we were still hyped-up from the move. It was also freezing cold because the house had been uninhabited and hadn't yet had sufficient time to warm through. We wondered aloud to each other what on earth we had done leaving behind our cosy little house for this large, cold one, a house with even more empty bedrooms, but also with lots of possibilities.

In the middle of all this we went to London for our Foresight screening tests. As well as my examination, which was like a cervical smear, Jeremy had another sperm test which showed the same results as before, a very high count but low motility. He was given vitamins to improve their health and I was treated for a Candida Albicans infection. Then I was given a tincture to help my cycles regularise, which did help to settle them down to a reasonable length. Along with that, the Persona monitor proved to me month after month that I was definitely ovulating.

Our lives became busier as the year went on. We attended our first Alpha Course and experienced a renewed enthusiasm for Jesus, especially as we both asked to receive the Holy Spirit for the first time. We completed our Scout Leader training after five years and were awarded our Wood Badges. We took our Venture Scouts on a very successful camp to the Lake District, were flooded out at the Scout Millenium Camp and attended a wonderful Pentecost 2000 celebration at the Three Counties Showground.

On the house front, we began to redecorate and also held a massive housewarming party for 95 people on the hottest day of the year (which was just as well, as we didn't actually have room for them in the house). Not surprisingly, I hardly wrote in my diary at all that year as our lives were very, very full. In the summer our good friends Sally and Michael left for a three year posting abroad. It was upsetting for us, but they were delighted to have the chance to achieve an ambition. We ran a fabulous Scout Camp in August. It was such fun that I laughed all week long and then as the autumn term began we plunged into rehearsals for a Pantomime written by a talented member of our Venture unit. Add to that Church, Housegroup, lots of visitors and a First Aid Course and we had a crazy schedule on our hands. As Christmas approached I had to admit that we had taken on too much, but at least that autumn I was too busy to sink into gloominess again.

Since my change of attitude early in the year I had put my trust more and more in God's plan for me and the more I prayed for His will to be done, the more encouragement I received from Him. Then, towards the end of the year, I had a very significant and exciting set of experiences while praying, related in my diary entry below:

14th November, 2000 (cont.) On the infertility side of things, I'm now undergoing a test to see if my problem is an inability to produce the hormone needed to hang on to a newly-fertilised egg. I've had proof of ovulation for an astonishing 7 months in a row but still am not pregnant and my cycles are still irregular, so Foresight are trying to find out whether I'm just unable to hang on to a baby. I must admit, I have wondered about this possibility before. I have to chew bits of cotton wool at various points of my cycle and then send them off to have the saliva analysed. I pray that this will shed light on the general mystery.

Apart from this my morale is good (there hasn't been time for it to be otherwise) and I've had four or five strong 'pictures' (like waking dreams or visions) which I hope are from God as I would very much like to put my trust in them. I can still see them as clearly as when they flashed into my mind at first.

One is of a page of this diary with the words 'I AM PREGNANT' written on it down at the bottom of a list of ovulation dates, one is of me with a baby in the bathroom drying it after a bath, one is of me walking along the common holding the hand of a toddler, and the most recent is of me lifting a child from a cot in the little bedroom. Whether these are true pictures or extreme wishful thinking only time will tell, but to be honest I'm treating them a bit like a promise from God that will be fulfilled at the right time and it helps me to control the frightening despair that sometimes still threatens to engulf me.

Another vision was of me sitting on a rocking chair in our smallest bedroom holding a baby over my shoulder. I couldn't be sure that they were promises from God and yet they had come into my mind with the same quiet authority I had experienced in the voice telling me that my work colleague was pregnant. All I knew was that the more I turned to God and prayed and tried to find out what He wanted of me the more wonderful and amazing experiences I had. It was so different from all the years I had spent insisting that God do things my way. The peace and joy that were the reward of my new attitude of humility were astonishing.

12th December, 2000 I should have written this yesterday but I ran out of time. I wanted to tell about how good God is to me and yesterday I was so brimful of joy that I was overflowing with it… On Sunday at Church we prayed for the Holy Spirit to fill us with love and the desire to spread God's word to the town and I can't say I felt particularly enthusiastic about it then. But on Monday morning as I walked through Priory Park and up Church Street to work, I suddenly found myself so full of joy that I couldn't help praising God for his goodness to me and really wishing that everyone I passed knew about Jesus. I felt such an urge to pray for everybody, so I did, very earnestly. It was joy like you feel when you're a child and it's Christmas, bubbling up uncontrollably. I'm so lucky that God bothers with me. Especially because my heart is often filled with that wonderful joy at my lowest times (when I find I'm not pregnant again) as if that is when He is most full of care for me. I understand now that being a Christian doesn't mean that hard times don't come, it means that you don't have to face them alone. The media represents Christianity as a passed phase, a dead thing, but love of Jesus was incredibly alive in me yesterday.

Finally in the mood to accept what God had to give me, the joy and peace He poured out on me at that time was abundant. And now I also had those visions to hang on to as another childless year came to a close. In a rare peaceful moment, I sat at my desk one day in December writing my Christmas list to give to my family. When I had finished thinking of a few things that they could easily give me, I turned it over and wrote on the back in two tiny words what I really wanted for Christmas, 'children' and 'time'. I asked God to grant my wish for children if it was according to His will and also to help me to calm down and manage my time better.

The Pantomine was a sell-out success, the First Aid course came to an end, the Scouts and Ventures all went off on their Christmas holidays and didn't need us any more. It was time to think about our own lives again, because the end of 2000 was our self-imposed deadline for a reconsideration of IVF. Eighteen months had passed since we were first told by the Consultant that he would refer us for IVF. During that time I had pursued the Foresight program of vitamins, worked hard, served the community and finally begun to learn to submit myself to God's will, but not one word had passed our lips about IVF. Jeremy waited patiently for me to be ready for the discussion without putting the slightest pressure on me and had in the meantime allowed me to foist all sorts of vitamins and unpleasant tests on him. But despite all of this, we had failed to conceive and seemed as far from having our own family as ever, even though I now felt that God had promised us children. And yet my attitude towards IVF was utterly unchanged. I was still very afraid of drugs interfering with my body and the more I immersed myself in the Foresight view of healthy living as an aid to conception, the more I considered IVF as horrifyingly unnatural. What's more, I knew God had the power to work a miracle and give me a baby just as He had done for my friend Laura and therefore IVF couldn't possibly be the way He was going to fulfill his promises. Could it?

Our schedule had calmed down considerably and we had more time on our hands, but even so I began 2001 carefully avoiding the IVF discussion. Instead, I decided to redecorate our bedroom. When that came to an end, I still did not feel ready to tackle the dreaded subject.

*28ᵗʰ **April, 2001** January was our deadline for deciding on IVF treatment but it came and went and I still couldn't face the subject AT ALL. Foresight offered me another tincture to normalise my cycles, so I took it for a while and continued to hope, and of course, kept praying. But I began to feel deeply frustrated again, and in early February I lay awake in bed one night sulkily accusing God of never helping me to make decisions as I've heard He helps other people.*

It wasn't much of a prayer. An accusation is a more accurate description of the things I said to God that night. I wasn't polite and I didn't use what we often consider to be the right sort of language for a prayer. In a silent diatribe I screamed my need for guidance to God and railed at Him for never making it clear to me what I should do. Why wouldn't He just tell me in the same way that He told people in the Bible at critical moments? It may have been said in the manner of a tantrumming child, but at least my message was baldly honest. My mind was in turmoil, I had reached another critical point and I simply couldn't cope any longer without God's direct help.

*28th April, 2001 (cont.) The next day, while Jeremy and I were driving down to Cirencester, I suddenly knew, with complete certainty from that moment onwards, that we **had** to go for fertility treatment. Jeremy was delighted as he had been quietly waiting for me to be ready for ages. We were even provided with time to discuss it away from our worldly cares because we were travelling. Once the decision was taken, and ever after since, I have felt utterly sure. This, from someone who couldn't even bear to think of it at all before! So I thanked God sincerely for responding to my rude request with such undeserved mercy and compassion.*

With God's help, the dreaded decision was faced and made in one moment. Where before there had been turmoil, indecision and a whole mind shouting 'No!', now I discovered peace, calm and assurance. Half-hearted acceptance would have been understandable, but instead I suddenly found that I could face the next stage of our quest for children wholeheartedly and with certainty. Only God could have affected that sudden and complete change of heart. And with Him guiding me on I knew it would be ok, that I could face anything. So it was all systems go. After eighteen months avoiding the subject entirely I suddenly felt that there wasn't a moment to lose! If God wanted me to go for IVF then I was going to step out in faith, even into what I most feared.

28th April, 2001 (cont.) I urged Jeremy to explore the Internet for IVF info and we found an excellent website that helped us to choose the hospital we wanted to go to, The Priory in Birmingham. My doctor immediately referred us and also offered to pay for one cycle of drugs, saving us about £600!

We had to bear most of the cost ourselves because I had never even allowed our names to be put on the waiting list for NHS funded treatment. Both sets of parents offered to give us some assistance, which was a great help. We consulted the Human Fertilisation and Embryology Authority website and chose the Priory because it was reasonably near to Malvern, it's results compared well with the other hospitals offering IVF and it was quite a small unit. I couldn't face being one among hundreds of women passed from one Consultant to another again, so this was a good decision for us. We discovered that based on other women in my age group (I was 29 at this point) our chances would be about 30%, which didn't sound much but was a great deal better than nothing. Jeremy found some useful websites, but when we went on to read exactly what was involved in IVF treatment, my first reaction was to sob my heart out. The drugs, injections, operations and other medical procedures that I would have to endure sounded horrible and just as unnatural as I had suspected. I was terrified, but God had given me His guidance and so I made myself go on as quickly as possible.

While reading up about fertility treatment on the internet, we were prompted to explore various moral issues surrounding the subject, including whether we would accept donated sperm or eggs if our own were not viable. I offer our prayerful conclusions here as an insight into our thought processes and not as a judgement on people who have made different decisions. In our thinking, we tried very hard to balance our own desperation for a child with the wellbeing of the potential child itself. So, one of my objections to IVF was the potential damage to a child that might result from being created in a test tube, but the information we read was reassuring. IVF children had shown no significant differences from other children and were of course created from the same basic materials, an egg and a sperm from their parents. The only difference was the way they were brought together. The intervention of the Embryologist alarmed me a little as he or she, rather than nature, would have to select the individual sperms, but I felt that ultimately, in answer to our prayers, God would be in control of the selection.

However, if our own basic materials were not viable, we made a unanimous decision not to accept donated eggs or sperm from other people and to abandon our attempts to achieve a pregnancy. Neither of us wished to seek deliberately to create a child adrift from its natural parents just to fulfill our own desire for a pregnancy, particularly when there already existed many children unable to live with their natural parents who were in need of a home. In the case of one or both of us being unable to be a natural parent, we decided to explore the possibility of adoption instead. Neither would we donate eggs or sperm to other couples, for the same reasons. The use of donated eggs and sperm was a legal possibility, but not, we felt, a moral possibility for us.

We also talked about how many cycles of IVF we would try before accepting that it was time to stop. Jeremy proposed three, which seemed a good number and just about affordable, so we agreed on three attempts. I could see, however, that if we tried unsuccessfully three times but there was still cause for hope, it would be very difficult to walk away from our only chance of a child and I wasn't convinced that I would be able to do so. However, it seemed like a good idea to have a limit in mind. Many more attempts than that would be financially ruinous in any case.

The last issue we discussed was what to do with any left over embryos, should we get that far in the process. Freezing technology offered a chance to store embryos so that further attempts to conceive were possible without having to go through the complete treatment cycle from scratch every time. On the down side, on average one third of frozen embryos were not expected to survive the freeze-thaw process, so we could expect to lose some of the embryos if they had to be frozen. On the positive side, however, children born from good quality embryos that had survived the freeze-thaw process had shown no significant differences to normally-conceived children. So we felt reasonably happy to agree to freezing any 'spare' embryos. What to do with embryos we did not wish to use was another question. They could be kept frozen for five years and then after that would be taken out of the freezer to perish (we are talking about organisms with only a couple of cells, too microscopic to see with the human eye). When we considered that within the normal human reproductive cycle, embryos are often created which then fail to implant and perish naturally, we both felt that allowing any unused embryos to perish was not too different to the natural way of things. The only real difference was that we would have to make a choice about it, not to mention the emotional difficulty of letting go of something we had struggled so hard to create.

While my mind was still reeling from these issues, the process began. Firstly we visited the Consultant at the Hospital to talk things through. He suggested at the outset that a less drastic treatment like I.U.I. (Intra-Uterine Injection) might be enough. On that visit we also had blood tests done to check for infections, rubella immunity, HIV, etc., and Jeremy had to have yet another sperm test. We didn't have to wait long for the results and when they came we unexpectedly received our first major blessing of faithfully embarking on IVF.

28ᵗʰ April, 2001 (cont.) Even the initial tests were utterly worthwhile because we finally found out why we haven't conceived in the past and why we aren't likely to without help. Jeremy has a problem with his sperm such that although he has a high count, 95% are of poor quality due to various factors like abnormalities and, most particularly, due to 'agglutination' – i.e. antibodies are present causing them to stick together. The results were so poor that the Consultant went from recommending I.U.I. (artificial insemination, not very intensive treatment) to I.C.S.I. (where a single sperm is injected straight into an egg, last ditch attempt treatment).

I was so taken aback when I received this information from the Embryologist that I didn't pause between phone calls. In floods of tears, I rang Jeremy and he came home from work so that we could sit and discuss this unexpected development.

28ᵗʰ April, 2001 (cont.) Oh my goodness! What a mix of feelings we experienced upon this news. Jeremy was angry at first. After all, he has never refused a test, so why couldn't they have told him this before? Then he was intensely relieved that we finally had an explanation. He is not the type of man to feel that his ego was damaged by the news, I'm glad to say. And I felt astonished, then relieved and then jubilant. After all, if the problem isn't me (now that my pill-related traumas are over) then surely we stand a good chance of responding to treatment? This was something really gained.

It truly was. Four years after our quest for children began we finally knew why we couldn't conceive. For four years I had endured tests, drugs, constant failures and great anguish as I lived with the assumption that it was entirely my fault that I hadn't become pregnant. I blamed myself constantly for failing to give Jeremy a child. Now in one afternoon it had all been wiped away. Instead of facing the unknown we faced the known. Instead of struggling with my infertility, it now looked as if I'd been normally fertile all along and we had just been confused by my bizarre responses to hormone drugs. Best of all, if the hospital could help us to overcome the actual problem, getting the sperm to the egg in the first place, it looked as if there should be no reason whatever that I couldn't successfully sustain a pregnancy.

For days I walked around in a state of total happiness because at last there was *real* hope. Of course, I also felt sad that Jeremy had the

Anti-Sperm Antibodies problem in the first place, but it didn't really figure when weighed against my pleasure at knowing what the problem really was after all the years of wondering. The team at the Priory could offer no real explanation as to why Jeremy had ASA. It could perhaps, they suggested, be due to an injury to that area of his body at some point in the past, which had caused his body to produce antibodies against itself. There appears to be very little research into this condition. But neither of us really cared. We simply accepted the fact gratefully because at long last that's just what it was - a fact.

5

We booked ourselves straight in to begin ICSI treatment. There were forms to fill in and a trip to the hospital to discuss the treatment with the Embryologist. We were warned that there were lots of unknowns, such as whether I would even respond to the stimulating hormones, and a few dangers like that of OHSS (Ovarian Hyperstimulation Syndrome). We were also offered counselling with a trained counsellor. I wasn't really worried by anything the Embryologist said. I had already faced up to the horribilities of it all and I just wanted to keep moving forward. Events moved on at such a pace that the diary entry from April was the first I had written that year. I had time to write then because Jeremy and I were on holiday, itself an answer to prayer.

28th April, 2001 We are staying in a lovely flat in Falmouth. It is right on the side of the estuary and from the fabulous window seat where I am currently ensconced, I can see boats anchored, the St. Mawes ferry coming and going, and all the way to Pendennis Castle. It's a lovely calming view and Jeremy and I have both spent many, many hours sitting here since we arrived on Tuesday. I'm so glad we came, I'm having a very happy time.

Usually we were unable to afford a holiday like that, but had been offered the flat for free by the company I worked for providing we could go at one of its unoccupied times. I was very pleased and excited to contemplate a holiday in luxury for once instead of in a tent, but we were just embarking on the treatment and suddenly the timing of all our plans was called into question.

28th April, 2001 (cont.) The initial tests and things happened during March. We had no idea when treatment would begin so we left alone our plans for Venture Camp to Snowdonia and this holiday. And then there was an outbreak of Foot and Mouth disease. I had no idea it would affect us all so much. I haven't been able to walk my normal route to work for weeks and all our Scout and Venture hikes and Wide Games had to be cancelled. It's been terrible for the poor farmers. One of the affects was actually fairly positive for us, though, as our Snowdonia camp had to be cancelled, relieving us of a great deal of stress and pressure at a time when we had been advised to take it easy.

Until my period began we still had no idea when the treatment would be, but rather than getting stressed about it, I prayed and handed all the things that were out of my control to God, knowing that His will for us would be best even if it seemed hard at the time. When I came on, it looked as though our holiday was entirely scuppered but – oh joy! – when I phoned the hospital they couldn't fit me in for egg collection until 8th May so our holiday was saved. Thank you Lord!

By the time we left for the holiday I had already been using a Buserelin sniffer for several weeks. It's purpose was to 'down-regulate' my system, switching off my ovaries and putting me into a false menopause, but it also had several very unpleasant side-effects on me. I experienced hot flushes, a racing heart and low moods. About four days after beginning it, I hit a terrible mood of gloom and anger. I picked a huge fight with Jeremy in the course of which I kicked the airing cupboard door so hard that I left on it a skid mark of black rubber from the bottom of my shoe! I really felt murderous. The fight blew over, Jeremy dutifully scrubbed the mark from the door and the next day my temper subsided to an irritable but controllable level.

The next stage of the treatment, once-daily injections of Gonal-F to stimulate my ovaries to produce plenty of follicles, was due to begin while we were away. Such was my fear of needles that my dread of the injections did hang rather oppressively over the start of our holiday. I had to continue with the sniffer so that my own hormones remained suppressed, but I had been told that the Gonal F would probably have a positive effect on my menopausal low mood. Jeremy shook as he put the first injection together, mixing the little vials with fumbling fingers, and I shook as he held an auto-injector onto my bottom and pressed the button which sent the needle stabbing in. It was unpleasant, but I still had that underlying sense of God's peace and I never wavered from my chosen path.

28th April, 2001 *(cont.) I still feel confident that this is what we should be doing and that whether it is God's will that it succeeds or fails He will help us to cope. I can also look back on the last 4 years now with no regrets. There's no point in wishing to be different. This is how we are and, oddly, we have gained so much by our infertility. Had I conceived years ago, would we have a Venture Unit? Would we have a flourishing Scout Troop? Would we have been able to move to our lovely house? And would I now have this trust in Jesus, this acceptance of His will for me? It's been so hard, but I wouldn't want to change it at all.*

30th April, 2001 *5 injections down and 7 to go! I shall be so glad when* *this bit is over. Here's another marvellous thing God did for me in the fertility saga. I hoped that we might find a Christian member of staff at the Priory Hospital as confirmation that we were in the right place. On our last visit we discovered that the Nurse who has guided our treatment so far is a Christian. It just came out in conversation. I felt so glad to know there was an ally in that place!*

Other things cropped up in a timely manner to help me through the weeks of treatment. Earlier in the year I had corresponded with a Professor of English Literature at the University of Western Australia who was interested in my Ph.D. work. He was asked by the editor of the *Encyclopedia of British Literature* to recommend someone to write entries for the Encyclopedia on two female Gothic novelists of the eighteenth century and he kindly put my name forward. I was given two writers to work on, Ann Radcliffe and Sophia Lee, and I thoroughly enjoyed the reading and research involved. The articles were due for submission by the beginning of June, so I was thoroughly occupied with them just as the treatment moved into the anxious stages. At work I was well supported by my boss.

30th April, 2001 (cont.) My boss has been awfully kind. Not only did he willingly give me lots of time off when I told him about ICSI, he has also given me extra paid holiday in which to recover.

As promised, a few days into the stimulating injections my mood began to improve considerably. The hot flushes stopped and I could definitely feel something happening in the region of my ovaries, similar to a normal ovulation but much, much stronger. Our holiday came to an end and I had to go straight to the hospital for a scan to see what my ovaries were up to. Had they responded adequately to the injections? I should have had the scan a day or so before but we had delayed it so that we could finish our holiday. The news we received as I lay in the little darkened room and the Nurse scanned me internally was startling, to say the least.

11th May, 2001 ... at my scan the Nurses were troubled to discover that I had a good 20 follicles on my ovaries (the average is 8) and became concerned that I was heading for Ovarian Hyper-Stimulation Syndrome (OHSS), which is a potentially unpleasant and even dangerous condition. They immediately halved my dose of the injected drug, but after another scan a few days later, which showed up even more follicles I was told to cease the injections altogether. I felt poorly. My heart kept racing, I felt very tired and a bit bloated. Given the state of my ovaries, the Nurses were quite surprised that I wasn't much more ill. So they 'coasted' me for a few days, basically allowing the Oestradiol in my blood to fall to safer levels. At least I'm fertile enough to produce so many follicles! I have been very good at looking on the bright side and staying very relaxed.

When I wrote this entry, I was mercifully ignorant of just how dangerous the condition of OHSS could be. Years later, through a news story on Woman's Hour, I learned that it is possible for over-stimulation of the ovaries to be fatal. They revealed details of a woman whose quest for children had tragically led to her death from OHSS. As I listened, I was overcome by the fear I was too ignorant to feel at the time, weeping for the poor woman who had died and for myself because of the dreadful things we both had to brave in order to have what others had so easily. Finally I understood why, back in 2001, the Nurses were so alarmed and why the concerned Consultant rang me at home at the weekend to check that I was drinking plenty and not having any difficulty breathing.

So there I was with OHSS. The bloating in my abdomen became very uncomfortable. If I laughed, it felt as if my shoulders were about to fall off. But I had been through so much weirdness already with the sniffer that I just accepted it as part of the treatment. The Nurses monitored me closely and finally the first stage of the treatment came to its conclusion. When the follicles looked big enough, I had my final injection of the ripening hormone and Egg Collection was scheduled for a precise time afterwards. The Nurses gave us just a few instructions at a time because there was no point worrying about the next stage of the treatment until the one before had proved successful. It was a good thing for me that they did, and that they gave handy reminder leaflets, as I felt so tired and confused that I could hardly take any of it in. It was a relief that the injections were all over, although I wasn't looking forward to the operation. It was performed under a general anaesthetic. While I was unconscious, the Consultant put a needle into each of the follicles on my ovaries and extracted an egg if there was one.

11th May, 2001 *I survived Egg Collection today. It was the worst bit so far, because we had to get up at 5 a.m. to be at the hospital for 6.30 a.m. and I had a general anaesthetic which left me feeling sick and wobbly. Also my ovaries were very painful afterwards, although I've had various painkillers since, so I'm feeling fine now. The good news is that from my 40 or so follicles, they managed to collect 23 eggs, which gives us an excellent chance of achieving enough healthy embryos to go on to the next stage. If they develop and I'm well enough, Embryo*

Transfer will take place on Sunday or Monday and that will only be as bad as a smear test, which is trifling compared to today's experience. We might even have enough embryos to store some in the freezer in case I don't get pregnant this time or for more chances later. Either way, it could mean that I will never have to go through the experiences of the last two weeks again, thank goodness. I'm so glad we didn't start this treatment until I felt emotionally ready and sure because it would have been even more stressful. As it is, I've remained very relaxed, working on my articles and taking it easy. Last night a huge bouquet of flowers arrived from work with a 'get well soon' card which made me miss them all. Jeremy has been so supportive, driving backwards and forwards to Birmingham, letting me cry all over him and fetching me drinks and food at unearthly hours!

While my Egg Collection operation took place, Jeremy had to provide a sperm sample, and then it was all handed over to the Embryologist, who selected what she smilingly called 'pretty sperm' to be injected into the eggs. We were very nervous waiting for the outcome of the attempted fertilisation and it was one of those moments when I was struck very strongly by the unnaturalness of the process. Fertilisation should be happening inside my body, I thought, not in a test tube. I overcame those negative thoughts by praying particularly hard that God Himself would guide the Embryologist's hand. I felt reassured that despite the circumstances, God was in charge and any embryos created would be works of His hand.

We were elated when 17 of the 23 eggs collected successfully fertilised. 17 embryos! Everything looked hopeful and we expected Embryo Transfer, where the two healthiest embryos would be put back into my womb, to take place imminently. But it wasn't to be. Because my ovaries were very swollen and my abdomen still bloated with fluid retention, I was judged to be too ill for the transfer to take place. Every one of our embryos had to be stored in a freezer and we were told we had to wait two or three months until I was well enough to proceed. Disappointment, frustration and fear swiftly replaced my earlier elation. It was a very strange time, as in a haze of illness I was buffetted by huge emotions. It was as if I was strapped to a rollercoaster that careered on its own scary path taking me wherever it would. All I could do was hold on tight and wait for the end of the ride.

I finished writing my articles while I recuperated and then my 30th birthday arrived. In more optimistic times we had planned a celebratory barndance, but when the day came I was too ill to participate, so I had to sit and chat and watch everyone else being energetic. I was still swollen round the middle, which wasn't quite the look I was hoping for on that occasion, but it was enjoyable nonetheless. I minded turning 30 less than I'd anticipated because I felt for the first time in years that we had just achieved a major step towards starting our family. Perhaps the decade ahead would see the fulfilment of my dearest hopes. It was an exciting prospect.

Once the swelling had gone down after a few weeks, I began to feel impatient to get on with the next stage. The Nurses thought I should wait a little longer but impatience drove me and I insisted on going ahead. They checked with the Consultant and I was allowed to begin a 're-implantation cycle', which involved going back on the dreaded sniffer to down-regulate my system again and then taking HRT tablets. The latter made me feel very low indeed, but the worst bit was adjusting to the sniffer again. This time the airing cupboard door was safe but I stood behind the car and asked Jeremy to run me over and I wasn't really joking. The strange moods were very hard to cope with and I leaned heavily on Jeremy for support.

6th July, 2001 This morning Jeremy had to make all my decisions for me as my brain had been replaced by cotton wool. Embryo transfer takes place on July 19th. Nearly there now.

God's support was also amazing. That morning I walked to work in a total daze, struggling to string a thought together, praying confusedly as I went, when I heard that calm voice in my head again.

6th July, 2001 (cont.) God is so good. At my lowest moment this morning I heard an authoritative voice tell me to read Romans 4. It meant so much to me when I did as it spoke of Abraham's trust in God and God's promise to Abraham and Sarah of a child.

I wasn't particularly well acquainted with the later books of the New Testament, so it was a complete surprise to me to read what Romans 4 had to say. It filled me with hope and trust again and made me think afresh about God's promises to me.

6th July, 2001 (cont.) I also prayed for a simple task to do at work and lo! an order came in for me to print 11 catalogues. Very mindless and quite perfect.

My boss was great. That day he noticed that I wasn't at all myself and discreetly slipped me a little note asking if I was ok and would I like him to run me home. I wrote in reply, "No thank you, I'm fine here, but aliens have stolen my brain." He grinned and left me to it.

When my body was prepared to receive the embryos, the most

nerve-wracking bit took place. Four embryos were taken out of the freezer and we had to hope and pray that they would survive the thaw and start dividing. The astonishing news was that all four survived and were doing so well that they were all considered to be Class 1! The best two were chosen and at last we went to the hospital for the Embryo Transfer. I had to lay on a bed with my legs in the air on rests and my bare bottom on display to the world. The two embryos were transferred into my womb in a procedure similar to a smear test. Jeremy sat up by my head and watched from a dignified distance. I lay and prayed and my heart was so full of joy I thought it would burst. I was so happy to have this chance, so glad that God had brought me safely through all the weirdness to this moment. I was wheeled into another room and then we were left alone so I could lay quietly for 20 minutes to let the embryos 'settle'. The Nurses checked I was equipped with the progesterone pessaries I now had to use twice daily to help my body hold on to a pregnancy, should the embryos happen to take. And then we went home and that was that. The 'long wait' had begun.

Six of those long, long days were taken up by Venture Camp near Southampton. The Nurses were a bit alarmed by the prospect of me going on the camp but I needed something to do and I promised to take things easy. I was very anxious over everything I did, though, worrying constantly in case I was harming the embryos by lifting a bag, walking around too much, eating the wrong thing. It was like all the worries I'd ever experienced over the years concentrated into this one short period. And I looked constantly for signs. I was terribly tired, which is not wholly unusual for a camp. I went to visit a friend who lived nearby and when she left her bed-sitting room to get something, I thought I would just lay my bleary head down on her pillow for a few minutes. I never made it as far as the pillow. I just fell asleep where I first leaned over and she left me in peace for several hours. I was tearful and moody, which is not surprising given the hormones I was still taking and the possibility of an impending period. I remember going to the loo block one morning to use a pessary. I leaned on the wall of the loo and wept, reflecting morosely on the pointlessness of it all. I would surely not be pregnant anyway, perhaps it just wasn't possible for me. I began to experience a lot of period pains. And then the night before the test, terror washed over me as I went to the loo and found a spot of blood. With a sinking heart, I had to accept that it hadn't worked.

And yet the next thing I wrote in my diary, underneath a very long list of ovulation dates and in the last available space in the otherwise full diary were the following amazing words:

I AM PREGNANT!

*It's **31ˢᵗ July, 2001** and today the hospital gave me a pregnancy test and I am pregnant! I really thought I wasn't, it's a miracle! Praise God from whom all blessings flow! I had a vision of this very diary entry, written in this exact place on this very page, and now it's come true!*

It makes me weep all over again to read those words where I wrote them that glorious day. It was the culmination of so much heartache, effort, hope and prayer and there it was, I really was pregnant, just when I had truly believed I couldn't be. I chattered non-stop all the way home in the car, but it took quite a long time for the news to sink in. I wanted to sing it aloud to the whole world, although obviously at only four weeks pregnant that wasn't terribly wise! God had kept His promise to me and the first vision had come true. Surely that meant I could put my full trust in the others. In a nice, new diary, I wrote,

8ᵗʰ August, 2001 *God has been so good and generous and faithful as to grant me the chance of a child after 4½ years of hopelessness and anguish. My last diary ended amazingly with the fulfilment of a vision I had had of 'I AM PREGNANT' written on the very page where it now lies. Wow! I am 5 weeks pregnant and full of anxiety, hunger and tiredness! When they told us at the hospital that the treatment had worked – FIRST TIME!!! – I simply couldn't believe it. Apparently it's quite common to bleed a bit and after that dreadful day it did stop. However, not knowing that, I prepared myself for the worst and got the best instead! Jeremy and I went straight out to celebrate, but then and ever since I have felt dazed. Jeremy has been quite calm, as always, with bursts of excitement. I have been disturbed 3 times during the night by ravening hunger, an urgent emptiness that gnaws, so that I now have snacks by the bed (dried apricots taste fab at 4.30 a.m.!). I'm also very tired and have had a few afternoon naps and can't contemplate much but sleeping after 8 p.m.! Today I have been so anxious about miscarrying, because I had strong pains during the night and subsequently dreamt over and over about waking up and finding myself bleeding. Horrid. Then the car had a warning light on so that I didn't dare drive it and* *when I travelled on the bus instead the lurching made me feel so sick. Got to work pale and shaky and one of my colleagues packed me in her car and drove me home again!*

I did worry, but on the whole my strongest feeling was one of joyousness to have good news at last to impart to my family, friends and Church family. My symptoms of tiredness and hunger made me want to laugh from the sheer wonder that it was me, ME, suffering from them! Instead of gloomily, endlessly pondering our infertility problem, it was over. Whenever I noticed a physical symptom I hugged myself with glee and felt a pang of excitement all over again. I was actually carrying the beginnings of a baby inside me at last. And how lovely at last to hear news of other friends pregnancies with genuine, unalloyed joy.

9th August, 2001 *Also amazing is the news we just heard from Liz [a University friend] that she is also pregnant and our babies are due within a day of each other!! We were both worried about passing on our news, me because Liz had a miscarriage earlier this year and she because our treatment might have failed. It was such a relief to realise that we could be delighted and excited together AND to find that we could share each stage because we're in the same state exactly. We've begun e-mailing each other with daily nausea/hunger stories!*

I can't help but feel that God is pouring out blessings on me. My friend Sarah is also pregnant and 14 weeks along! She rang a few days ago after putting off telling me for fear of upsetting me and was so relieved and pleased to hear my news. I'm so glad not to make pregnant people feel guilty about telling me their news any more. Thank you, thank you, thank you Lord! Even if this pregnancy doesn't last everything is better than before because I AM A WOMAN WHO CAN GET PREGNANT!! After 4½ years of despair and frustration, I now know that it is possible for me to get pregnant and carry a baby at least for a little while. This makes a huge difference to me psychologically. Here's another good thing. Jeremy and I have had over 7 years of happy married life together before starting a family (8 by the time it's born), which a lot of folks don't get. I haven't really anything to complain of.

6

Those first couple of weeks of my long-awaited pregnancy were happy and exciting and most of the time I felt exuberant. But at 6 weeks I had another little bleed which sent me to the phone in a panic to receive reassurance from the hospital. The Nurse advised me to rest and try not to worry as it could just be caused by the embryo embedding into the womb lining. I went straight to bed and luckily the bleeding wasn't repeated. But after that I began to feel extremely nauseous. Even the smell of food made me retch and everything I ate tasted strange. I was also feeling exhausted, flopping onto the sofa after work and finding myself unable to get back up again for long stretches of time. Reluctantly, we made the decision that Jeremy should go and run Scout Camp by himself, assisted by a rota of other leaders. My parents came to stay with me. Two days after Jeremy left for camp I was violently sick and after that my physical symptoms went rapidly downhill with the rest of that month disappearing in a haze of illness. I was too weak to go to work and I struggled to keep any food or water down.

28ᵗʰ August, 2001 ... haven't written for a couple of weeks because I've been so ill and still am really. I am now actually being sick as well as feeling it all day. It's horrible. The rest of the time my stomach feels like a pit of boiling oil. Very unpleasant. I can't really go anywhere due to fear of throwing up and also, insanely, a constant hunger even though I can't stand the sight of food. People tell me it's a good sign and will only last till 12 weeks. I'm at 8 weeks now, so that currently seems a long way off.

Trying to be upbeat for a minute, the marvellously wonderful news is that I'm expecting TWINS!!! We found out at 6½ weeks when they scanned me and saw that both embryos had implanted and both had heartbeats. We saw the heartbeats! Just a tiny flicker, but definitely there. It was amazing. I didn't know whether to laugh or cry, so I did both. We are delighted and also very scared! Of course, this is one of the reasons that I'm feeling so bad. Two babies, two lots of hormones. My one aim each day is to get down enough food and fluid to keep me out of hospital, otherwise they'll take me in and put me on a drip.

I was amazed and delighted at the idea of twins! After so long waiting, an instant family seemed like a brilliant thing. But, sadly, moodwise I was at the beginning of a long slide down and all I could really hang on to was the idea that at least if I could have two babies at once I would never have to put myself through this awfulness again. I felt so ill that my whole life had come to a grinding halt. A Doctor visited and diagnosed Hyperemesis, offering me anti-sickness pills which I agreed to despite my general fear of drugs, grasping at anything that might make each day more bearable. I couldn't go to work, Scouts, Church or Housegroup, I couldn't shop, cook or clean. I just lay feeling terrible and wishing each day would pass quickly, trying to find things to distract myself but often falling asleep after a few minutes of activity or even mid-sentence. I read frantically any book that came to hand in order to take my mind off how I felt. I dreaded every meal and yet knew I had to try to eat and keep it down for the sake of the babies and to stop myself losing weight. I am a very small person, 5ft 1½" tall and 8 stone at the beginning of the pregnancy, and I was desperate not to lose too much weight. I was also struggling with a terrible anxiety over when I would be sick because it happened at least once a day and it always came upon me unexpectedly. I was afraid to go anywhere without a bucket at the ready and I was reluctant to see anyone in case I was sick in front of them.

It was hard for Jeremy, too, as he shouldered my usual jobs in the house, worked full-time and ran the Scout Troop and Venture Unit by himself. I lost interest in everything and lay alone on the sofa clinging to a book for all I was worth, wondering how to make it through each day. Time hung very heavily indeed on my hands and yet I felt too ill to do anything about it. My parents were great. Mum began to come over regularly in the middle of the week for a few days to keep me company and help out in the house. Only a few things from the outside world pierced the fog of gloom that was settling over me and unfortunately they were things that added extra layers of horror and sadness to my mood.

11th September, 2001 *I've been meaning to write for a while but HAD to today because of what has happened. As I sat on the sofa feeling queasy and listening to the radio, terrible news stories began to appear. Two aeroplanes crashed into the World Trade Centre in New York, destroying both towers and probably killing thousands of people. What's more they were hijacked passenger planes, so all of the passengers were killed, too. A third hijacked plane crashed into the Pentagon, again killing passengers and people in the building, and a fourth crashed in Pennsylvania. And a car bomb went off in Washington, too. I listened in complete astonishment and horror. The thought of what all the innocent, unsuspecting people must have suffered is unbearable. I thought, what kind of a world am I bringing my children into? What if there's a war as a result of these atrocious actions? Will the Americans seek justice within the law, or will they be angry enough to fling a few missiles around? Heaven help us.*

I wrote a lot more, none of it different from what anyone else was thinking, I'm sure. The need to write about what I'd just heard prodded me out of my lethargy and into a description of my own state at that point.

11ᵗʰ September, 2001 (cont.) Despite the anti-sickness drugs I'm still being sick at least once a day and I feel unwell all day long. I am able to eat more, so my weight hasn't fallen any further than 7½ stone. I'm 10 weeks along now, so only a couple more to go until the placentas are working, the babies are fully formed and hopefully I will feel less sick. I've stopped worrying about miscarriage as I've been told about a billion times that sickness means safety for the babies because they are throwing out plenty of hormones or something. All I know is that these have been the longest 4 weeks of my life and I just want the sickness to end so that I can start getting excited about the fact that we're finally going to have children of our very own. I still can't really believe it.

God bless my Mum. She has been here on and off for the last 4 weeks, feeding me, cleaning my house, distracting me when I needed it and holding my hair out of the way while I threw up. She has shopped, fed the cats, cooked our tea, washed for us and sat with me whenever I needed her. She makes me feel safe in her presence and I feel homesick when she goes. If I can be even half as loving to my own children, I will think myself a successful mother. What would I do without her? What I want more than anything is to present her with two grandchildren who will adore her like I do. Mum is very good at quietly working out what most needs to be done and doing it. She doesn't make a fuss or tread on anyone's toes, she just helps.

After a month, I managed to struggle back into work but the feelings of sickness, weakness, dread and anxiety didn't go and I felt completely out of control. At last I reached the magic 12 weeks, still clinging on to everyone's assurance that the sickness would abate, and came off the Progesterone pessaries (the last part of the fertility treatment) but nothing really changed. The 12 week scan was a high point in an otherwise rather bleak time.

26ᵗʰ September, 2001 At least I feel a bit more confident that the babies will be ok. Yesterday I had a scan and it was such a joy to see my little ones for the small, perfectly formed babies they are now. A great relief, too, to know that they are growing well and at about the same rate as each other. It was amazing to watch them move around, twitch and throw their little hands out suddenly as if waving to us. Mum and Dad came as Jeremy had a meeting in London and they emerged from the room beaming. My babies are ok! Praise the Lord!

Unfortunately, there was more bad news to come that September. One of our university friends had a climbing accident on Ben Nevis and was killed instantly. He left behind him a wife, also a good friend, and an eighteen month old son. In between bouts of sickness, I managed to speak to her and a few of our other friends on the phone, but I was too ill to make it to the funeral. I wish I had been able to offer her more support. I tried to pray about it all, but it was very hard. My body was suffering, but what was even worse was what was happening in my mind. Just then, God seemed very far away from me indeed.

Still feeling sick and anxious, I was also starting to feel desperate for normality. I tried to pick up some of the dropped threads of my life, like going to Ventures once a week, but I was so tired and foggy in the mind that I felt unable to participate properly or engage my brain even to feel a genuine interest. It was as if I existed on a different plane from the rest of the world and I couldn't fathom how to get back to reality. One evening I tried going to Housegroup but I fell asleep during the Bible study, woke up towards the end feeling dreadful and was then sick. Everyone was very kind but the experience left me unhappy, drained and more anxious than ever. Worst of all were the feelings that began to assail me when I was alone during the day, particularly in the long afternoons after work.

17th October, 2001 Something that has been awful in the last week has been a feeling compounded of a mixture of despair, anxiety, boredom, frustration and fear. When it descends on me I just feel that everything is wrong with the world, there is something missing or awry that I just can't sort out. Sobbed my heart out 3 times today for no reason other than that awful feeling. It's like the weepy bit of PMT, but going on and on. I suppose what makes me most anxious is having no idea when the sickness and awful feelings are going to end. Some people are ill right through their pregnancies and it's that notion that I can't bear the thought of because it makes me feel trapped. I'm at 15 weeks now so it could ease any time and every day I wake up and hope but every day so far is the same.

Then the 'all's wrong with the world' feeling became much worse and even the relief I had experienced sinking into bed at night was at an end. A terrible anxiety began to keep me awake, flooding my body with a horrid feeling like a spreading poison and causing my heart to race so fast that I could not slow it down. Even trying to think positively and relax made no difference and I found myself awake and on the verge of total panic into the early hours of the morning and on into the day. Added to that was a total lack of motivation, so that although I had an extreme sense of frustration if I had nothing to do, I was utterly unable to motivate myself to undertake even the simplest task. Unmotivated, terrified to do anything, terrified not to, unable to sleep… it was all quite the opposite of my usual self. It was almost as if my pregnancy had triggered not just physical changes but a total reversal of character and I felt disorientated and anchorless. Every day brought fresh terrors that I no longer knew how to face.

30ʰ October, 2001 …it is a real effort to write to you today. For two days after I last wrote I was too afraid to be alone in the afternoon, so I sought refuge with Caroline one afternoon and Helen the next. The following day we were supposed to be going to a wedding and that night I had anxiety attack after anxiety attack and hardly slept at all. Panicked even about getting out of bed in the morning and facing the day. Once I made it to the shower I suddenly felt stronger, so we decided to go to the wedding. It took us 5 hours to get there because of the volume of traffic on the road and we missed the actual ceremony but we were in time for the photos. I was sick twice, but it was worth it because it was lovely to see everyone.

I feel pretty terrible all the time, but the anxiety is now far worse than the physical feelings. On Monday Jeremy went to Germany for a conference and Mum came to stay. I was in a bad way when she arrived. That Monday was the first time that I felt the babies move, at 17 weeks, a tickly, fluttery sensation which made me smile and feel glad for a little while.

With Mum there, I felt a little better, but the night before she was due to go home was terrible, one of the worst of my life. I was woken by floods of anxiety and terror and my mind turned desperately to thoughts about getting rid of the babies or myself so that it would stop, thoughts that the real me, still there somewhere, found abhorrent. It was unbearable, I didn't want to go on and could only beg Jesus to help me.

In the morning I told Jeremy and Mum all about it because I was now scared of myself and what I might feel driven to do if left alone again. Helen rang to see if I was alright as she was worried and when she heard how desperate I was feeling she said that she would contact

Ali (the host of our housegroup and a Consultant Psychiatrist) and would also pray for me. We then phoned the duty Midwife and she was great, listening carefully and taking me very seriously. During the course of the morning, she visited me with a Doctor and they recommended that I needed to see a Psychiatrist but recognised that it was also important to try to get the sickness under control as that was obviously at the root of the problem. They told me to stop taking the anti-sickness drug Stemetil as it wasn't doing any good and might even have unhelpful side effects. I was nervous about coming off, but actually noticed very little difference when I did, which goes to show that it wasn't actually doing much.

We all agreed that it was important for me not to be left alone, so I went back home with Mum. Just like before, I felt jumpy, distracted, frustrated and exhausted. It was almost as if I was wired up wrong and when I ought to take the chance to relax I got really worked up instead. Jeremy drove over after work, so I was surrounded by my family which made me feel safer. The next day I began a new anti-sickness drug which I took from then until the end of the pregnancy. For the first time in months I almost enjoyed my lunch but I was still sick right before we left to go home. Peaceful sleep, peaceful rest, peaceful enjoyment of food all seemed wholly out of my reach and my state of panic so normal that I could hardly remember what it was like to be the pre-pregnancy me.

Mum came home with us, to my great relief, as I was still terrified to be alone. We went together to see the Psychiatrist, who diagnosed me with severe depression. She said I would have been sent to the Psychiatric unit at the hospital if Mum had not been able to stay with me. She was keen to try me on anti-depressants and I agreed, though I was extremely apprehensive. It felt good to talk it all through with an understanding professional who seemed to recognise and have a name for the dreadful things that were happening to me and I felt better and more positive for the rest of the day. Even better still, I wasn't sick.

However, the next day was a disaster and remains imprinted on my mind as a traumatic experience. I was too scared to get out of bed in the morning, but Mum and Jeremy talked me through it and encouraged me along. Then I reluctantly and amid tears took my first anti-depressant. An hour after taking the tablet I was sick. A bit later I was sick again. And then again. During the course of the day I was sick 5 times and I felt absolutely terrible. I couldn't go to work or out at all, all I could do was sit and feel ill and anxious. At one of the lowest moments, I remember realising that I no longer knew how to smile or laugh. Then a memory of an incident at Scouts that I found hysterically funny at the time floated into my mind. Although I was unable to raise a smile, at least it reminded me that joy and laughter were actually possible and I held on to that thought like a drowning woman grasping a lifebelt. Meanwhile, my sense of frustration grew and grew. I couldn't keep any food down at all, which made me anxious about the babies and when we finally went to bed I couldn't sleep for anxiety attacks. I tried relaxation tapes, music, reading, but nothing worked, I just could not unwind.

By the next morning, I had decided that it was unsafe for me to experiment with any more anti-depressants because my system was so sensitive; it was unbelievably unhelpful to run the risk of really extreme nausea as a side effect and the extra anxiety it caused me on behalf of the babies was only likely to plunge me deeper into depression. The Psychiatrist agreed and offered instead to add me to the long waiting list for a place on an anxiety management course. Then I felt despair, because I could not postpone my hour of greatest need till the place became available. My hour of need was now. That afternoon I phoned Ali for advice. She thought that a course of intensive talking therapy (Cognitive Behaviour Therapy) would be my best hope to begin to claw my way back out of depression. She said that it was imperative for me to be on my way to mental fitness before the babies were born as what I would then have to cope with would be even more mentally and physically taxing. Then, out of her loving Christian heart, she offered her own services to me for free, to begin immediately, and I gratefully took the helping hand she offered.

7

It is difficult to communicate to someone who has never experienced it just how depression affects the mind beyond your conscious control. I know now that it is a physical illness resulting from a chemical imbalance in the brain, but at the time I could not understand why it was so difficult to fight my way out of it. Whether I was vulnerable to depression because of the powerful drugs that I had taken recently, whether it was because I was still ill with OHSS or whether it was simply the fact that I felt horribly sick for so long, I will never know. What I do know is that living through every minute of a severe depression unmasked by antidepressants was terrifying. When I woke in the morning, a gloom settled suffocatingly over my spirits so that the day ahead seemed like a huge, dark, fearful thing that I could not face. When Jeremy talked me gently out of bed and into the shower, my heart pounded with terror as if I was the victim in a horror movie. And yet around me everything was normal. The horror was only inside my own head. I felt a constant urge to run and hide, but there was nowhere I could go to escape from my own hideous thoughts. A terrible dread would descend upon me even while I was trying to engage with everyday tasks like the washing up. All I could do was crouch beneath the weight of it, feeling helpless and totally unable to lift it alone.

However, I could now accept that it wasn't just a case of 'pulling myself together' because I had an illness that would take time to recover from. And I could now try to focus on getting better. To become myself again was a long and difficult wade through deep waters, but each day, with encouragement, they became a little, a very little, shallower. I began the Changeways course with Ali, one session a week ending with prayer, and although I was initially dubious about it, it truly helped, both increasing my understanding of depression and equipping me painstakingly to build my own psychological defences against it. One of my early discussions with Ali reminded me how beneficial writing had always been to me in the past, so she encouraged me to write every day about how I felt. She also encouraged me to make a list of any experiences that had *ever* made me feel positive and then to use the list to help me start to seek positive experiences every day. It was like drawing up a personal map to navigate by in times of mental emergency. To begin with, none of the things I tried felt at all positive, but Ali had warned that they wouldn't and that I must just go on trying anyway. For weeks my writing was full of terror and a sense of bleak pointlessness, but gradually small points of light began to appear.

9th November, 2001 Last night I actually went to Scouts and we ran a Wide Game on the Common. Perhaps some people would think that a pregnant woman sitting on a barrel in the middle of a gorse bush at 8 p.m. on a freezing cold night is the real insanity, but I felt so much better for it and came home remembering the beauty of the stars and the dark outline of the hills and the excited shouts of the boys.

17th November, 2001 The babies are ok because I can feel them moving around several times every day, a sort of wriggling inside which I really like. I do love them so, even though I would like the pregnancy to be over.

And where did faith feature in all of this? At the time God felt far, far away from me and I couldn't quite believe that He had led me into this situation. I can't deny that I felt great resentment towards Him. I never lost my faith, I always knew that He was there, but I did have a hard time understanding why He blessed me with the longed-for pregnancy only to let me be so ill that it felt anything but a blessing. This was when I truly began to understand that being a Christian was not a guarantee for a suffering-free life, as Jesus's own life proved. I had stepped out in faith to find my path strewn with thorns and all I could do was trust that God would not allow me to be pushed beyond my endurance. Suddenly I found I couldn't sing Christian songs about being broken or moulded without bursting into tears. I now knew what the breaking process felt like and it wasn't something I would ever lightly ask for again.

Afterwards, I could clearly see how God carried me through the whole horrible experience, surrounding me with everything and everyone I needed to survive. Wonderful Ali tackled my broken mind, amazing Mum, Dad and Jeremy cared for my overloaded body, and any gaps were filled by loving members of my Church family. When fear drove me out of my house, they were the ones who took me in. When I was ill and alone, they were the ones who came alongside me. I am so grateful to them all. For a time, Helen kept me company every Thursday night while Jeremy was at Scouts, despite how hard it must have been for her to be confronted with my pregnancy. We talked, or she would calmly lift my hair out of the way while I was sick before emptying my bucket ready for the next time. She even started bringing her ironing so that I wouldn't feel beholden to her for giving me so much of her precious time. She said that it was good for her to set aside her time like that to get on with an onerous chore. I hated having to lean on other people and accept help, but they made it so easy for me with their sensitivity. The Doctors did their best, but it was my family and Church family who really saved me. I will never forget the uplifting feeling of love that surrounded me the morning I finally made it to Church, accompanied by Mum and Jeremy and my constant terror of being sick in public. When my name came up in the prayers, I felt so cared for. Even people who I didn't know too well at Church showed their care. One morning I received a card from an elderly lady. The card read, 'This too shall pass,' which was just what I needed to hear that day.

For a long time, I woke every morning and experienced the terrible sinking heart. Every day as my mind began to scream, 'I can't cope,' I had to start all over again combatting it with, 'I can cope,' as the Changeways course instructed me. I began to rediscover the positive. Going to work helped. Going to Scouts and Ventures helped. Going to Church helped. Seeing friends helped. Laughing helped immensely and also having a good cry. Particular Bible verses really helped, like Philippians 4:6, 'Do not be anxious about anything, but in everything, by prayer and petition, with thanksgiving, present your requests to God' (NIV). That verse became part of my treatment and I wrote it out on a scrap of paper and carried it everywhere with me to glance at for reassurance. I talked and talked about how I felt, and wrote everything down. When I look back on those days, they may be unfailingly grey in my memory; when I look at photos of myself and my ever-growing belly, I may notice most of all the deadness in my eyes; but I know that God was piecing me back together, remoulding me slowly, lovingly and faithfully.

And, as always, His timing was perfect. By the beginning of 2002, Mum and Dad were living with us for a part of every week and they had begun to ponder the future, not just in terms of helping me through the rest of my pregnancy but also in terms of how much support I would need after the babies were born. Their cottage was still on the market and all of a sudden everything came together. It was a complicated scenario, but exactly when we needed them the right buyers appeared and simultaneously a house only one street away from us in Malvern became available. It needed updating but the location was perfect. We wouldn't be living on top of one another and yet Mum and Dad could walk down an alleyway straight to our house in just 2 minutes, or a 45 second run in a crisis! Another of my worries subsided. If my parents were there to help me, I would surely be able to look after my babies properly despite my struggle with depression. During the last months of my pregnancy, builders moved in to make the house habitable for them.

The greatest blessing of all was that despite the fact that twin pregnancies are classed as high risk, my babies were doing brilliantly, growing well, moving about in a reassuring manner and in all ways showing normal development. I had regular scans every four weeks until 28 weeks and then every fortnight after that. I worked until 34 weeks, mainly because I was too afraid to give up and find myself with swathes of blank time in front of me. My back held out remarkably against the strain of carrying an enormous load. I became huge, gaining four stone in all (which was half my total body weight again), and I did find it very hard to move about towards the end. However, Mum and I discovered ways of allowing me to get out and about as it was an important part of my treatment to seek positive experiences each day. In the last few months my tummy became so huge that I could no longer reach the pedals of our car, so Mum took over the driving. I did my supermarket shopping from a wheelchair pushed by Mum. We also discovered the brilliant Shopmobility scheme in Worcester which allowed me access to an electric wheelchair. Once I discovered that they had variable speed control and I could crank up the power, I thoroughly enjoyed zooming about the shopping centre and streets (although cobbles posed a challenge) with Mum scurrying after me and I only ran over her feet twice (sorry, Mum!). Seeing life from the vantage point of a wheelchair was an educative experience as it noticeably changed people's attitudes towards me.

Sleeping became more uncomfortable as I could only lay on my side and it took an unbelievable effort to shift from one side to the other. The sheer weight of the babies pressing down on me if I tried to lie on my back left me struggling for breath. I had fluid retention and in the last few weeks lost sight of my ankle bones altogether underneath a thick layer of puffy skin. I found that swimming was a great help both in reducing the fluid retention and taking the appalling weight off me for a while and I went once a week, although it became harder and harder to reach my feet and legs to dry them afterwards. In all ways, it was a strangely magnified version of a normal pregnancy.

A few months before the babies were due we joined an NCT class and met a lovely group of people. I was the only one expecting twins but luckily for me our teacher had five year old twins herself and was very helpful to us. The class was great because it signalled the beginning of my long-awaited new life. Suddenly the focus shifted firmly beyond the dreadful pregnancy as we began to discuss childbirth, feeding, nappy changes and similar foreign concepts. It was also the beginning of a new social life. I hadn't yet made up my mind about whether to go back to work or not. Before the pregnancy I assumed I would give up work and be a full-time mother. During the depression, I so mistrusted my own feelings that I came to the conclusion that it was better to keep my options open. If I felt trapped at home and it sent me down into worse depression again it might be helpful to be able to go to work for a positive change. Alternatively, when I came back to myself I might wish to pursue full-time motherhood as I had planned. Either way, my new NCT friends meant that life as a Mum would be a sociable business.

The last few weeks of the pregnancy were very hard indeed. I still felt sick, meals were still difficult and I still threw up occasionally. Plus, I was so large and so tired that I could hardly think straight. The days felt very strange, although I was pretty used to living through strange days by then. We tried to sort out baby clothes and equipment but I couldn't even grasp the simplest concepts like how the sizes of baby clothes worked. How was newborn different from 0-3 months? How much of each thing did we need? I worried that my brain had turned to mush and I would never recover. A tide of stuff began to take over the house and I was too confused to bring any organisation to bear. I caught a horrid cold that would not go, had Carpal Tunnel Syndrome in my hands which rendered them stiff and painful every morning and I badly pulled a muscle in my left shoulder as I tried to lever my huge bulk out of bed one morning a week before I gave birth.

Through all of this, however, my mood remained reasonable and my 'team' – Ali, Jeremy, Mum and Dad - were helping me to prepare myself mentally for what was to come. The babies were still doing well but were wedged into awkward positions which were not at all promising for a natural birth. Twin One was stuck at the bottom in the breach position. Twin Two was wedged across its sibling's head in a transverse position. Neither of them had moved for weeks because they had simply run out of space. My pregnant stomach was vast and now reminded me of some alarming photos in a book about twin pregnancy that I had seen months before. Photo 1 was the rounded stomach of a woman carrying a singleton. Photo 2 was the whale-like extension of a woman carrying twins. It had filled me with terror when I saw what I was heading into, but by the end of the pregnancy my main reaction to my own appearance was astonishment. It seemed quite likely to me that I would literally burst. All in all, it was a relief when the Consultant recommended that I have a Caesarean Section, because then I knew exactly what I was facing and even when it would take place. The date was fixed for March 21st and I would be 37 weeks and 2 days along. The end was in sight and although I had to brace myself for abdominal surgery and then the demands of two newborn babies I faced it all with increased courage because at last the traumas of the pregnancy would be over and if the situation was still hard, at least it would be completely different.

Just before the end of the NCT course, one of the group gave birth to her baby and brought him along to a session. We suddenly realised that we were going to have *two* of those funny little things to deal with, causing us to exchange alarmed glances. But it also made me feel more curious about the little ones inside me. My thoughts had been consumed with myself and my own daily struggle to survive for so long that I hadn't been able to think much about the babies as individuals. As I looked at the first NCT baby I began to wonder just who my babies would be, what they would look like and who they would take after. It was a natural feeling of maternal curiosity and excitement and I enjoyed it. It reminded me that life wasn't going to be exclusively about me for very much longer. The focus was about to shift onto the babies and I was deeply, deeply glad.

Early on the 21st March, Mum and Dad nervously saw us off for the Royal Worcester Hospital. I think I prayed a bit, but it was still hard to pray, so I trusted that others were praying for me. The

Hospital was brand new, having opened only 4 days previously, and my babies were due to be the first twins born there. I was given a very nice single room equipped with two Special Care Baby Units just in case. I was visited by various Midwives and the Surgeon and then a very jolly duo of Midwives tried to lead us to the Operating Theatre. I say tried, because the hospital was new, the corridors were confusing and we made several visits to wrong rooms before locating the right one. Jeremy had to wait outside while I was given the spinal block injection. When I could no longer feel my lower body, he was allowed to come in and sit by my head. We were neatly protected from the business end of things by a screen and I felt no pain at all, only a bizarre rummaging sensation.

I cannot read this part of the story without welling up because from that time forth we ceased to be a childless couple. After five long years, we became parents to the loveliest little babies. At 9.36 a.m. 'Twin One' came into the world.

"It's a girl!" the Surgeon called and shortly afterwards Jeremy was handed a little bundle with a lot of dark hair and a beautiful sleepy little round face.

"That's Hattie," I smiled at Jeremy. While I was gazing at her, another rummaging commenced and at 9.38 a.m. 'Twin Two' was born.

"It's another girl! She's a redhead!" called the Surgeon.

I grinned at Jeremy and said, "That's Kay." She was held up for our inspection and we saw her sweet elfin features. And there they were at last, our daughters. It was an awesome moment.

We had known for a while that we had two girls on the way, so the names were all prepared. Mercifully, both babies were pronounced fine. Harriet Susan weighed in at 6lbs 7½ oz and Katherine Elizabeth weighed in at 6lbs 3½ oz, so they both made a brilliant start with no need of special care. I was wheeled into a side room to recover before returning to the ward. Hattie was tucked in beside me, Jeremy cuddled Kay, and I lay and felt jolly proud of myself for producing two such amazingly beautiful and healthy babies.

To say that my depression and all the difficulties of the preceding months were swept away in those precious moments would be just too cheesy and, frankly, untrue. There were still a lot of hard experiences to come. But as I look back on that day, a great change certainly occurred. The grey months were over. From that day onwards I began to notice the sunshine, in fact it seemed to shine non-stop all spring and summer-long that year. The feeling of holding my own children in my arms was incredible. Jeremy, who had been stoic all through, was more emotional than I had ever seen him before. Like most mothers, I looked at my little girls and wondered if the world had ever seen such beautiful and marvellous children. But the five years of difficulties we had fought through to get to this point made it all the more amazing. Those two little girls were and are the most precious things the world could ever have to offer and I thanked God for them from the very bottom of my heart. It was only when I began to look back at the beginning of our quest for children years later that I remembered the blithe words of the Nurse recommending a Spring baby, for the longest time an impossible goal, and realised that God's blessing poured out on me that day was a gift of joyful, miraculous, crazy abundance, for there we were at last with not one but *two* babies, born on the very first day of Spring!

8

My parents shot up to the hospital to visit and the four of us gazed at the new additions to our family with great jubilation, both that they had arrived safely and that as a team we had made it through to this point. But later that evening everyone left and I found myself alone in my darkened hospital room, spaced-out on morphine, wired up to a drip and a catheter, with two little babies bundled up in a basin just out of my reach. I couldn't get out to them, I couldn't hold them both safely in bed with me in case I fell asleep and dropped them, I didn't know what I was supposed to do with them, so I just lay in terror listening to their snuffling noises and wondering if they were choking. The Midwives came in occasionally and responded to my calls, but what I really needed was not to be left alone at all. So I lay in the dark with wave after wave of panic washing over me all night long.

We'd agreed that Jeremy should go to work while I was in hospital in order to save his leave for when we came home, so Mum was my first visitor the next day. By the time she arrived, I was in a terrible state and knew I could not face another night like the last. Mum went and asked the Midwives if she could stay with me overnight and they informed her that it was against the rules. Like me, my Mum is not a very assertive person, but the time had come to make a stand. She told the Midwives very firmly that she had just spent the last five months supporting me out of a suicidal depression, that until last night I had been accompanied day and night, that in addition we now had two babies to care for and she was not going to stand by and allow me to sink back into a depression because they had a rule to stick to. What's more, I was in a single room, so there was no possible way that she could inconvenience or disturb anyone by staying and if she was prepared to sleep on a chair in order to make sure I had the care I needed that was her business. The Midwives conceded defeat. Thank you, thank you, thank you God for my mother. What kind of state I would have been in after five panic-filled nights alone, a depressed, inexperienced mother with two babies to care for after major abdominal surgery, I simply dread to think. I didn't have to find out, however, because my heroic Mum was there.

The next dilemma was feeding. I dearly wanted to breastfeed and I tried and tried, but there were two major problems. One was that as I hadn't gone into labour naturally my milk didn't come in for a good seven days, so I had nothing for the babies apart from colostrum and they were getting very hungry. The other was that while Hattie latched on beautifully, Kay just couldn't seem to get the hang of it and my nipples were hurting so much after a couple of days and the loss of a whole layer of skin that I began to get disheartened. The Midwives and Breastfeeding Advisor tried their best, but every different Midwife coming onto her shift offered a different solution and I was confused and worn out as well as in discomfort from the Caesarean. At the end of my five days in hospital I still had no milk and the babies were being fed on formula through tubes attached to my breasts (we really did try everything) in order not to destroy my chances of breastfeeding altogether. Novel, but not very sustainable. On the other hand, there were so many positives to keep me going. The sight of my daughters and the joy of holding them were a constant delight. Another source of joy was the rediscovery of the pleasure of food! With the birth, the nausea came to an end and my appetite truly returned.

Jeremy came every evening while Mum popped home and did everything he could to help. He was besotted with his little daughters and had also lain awake most of their first night from sheer excitement! He did the first nappy changes and cuddled them for hours so I could rest. And the babies themselves were endlessly interesting when I wasn't struggling to feed them. They began to display quite different personalities even in the first few days of their lives. Baby Hattie would wail plaintively when she needed attention, rending the heartstrings, while Baby Kay's glass-shattering shrieks turned her whole head an explosive shade of scarlet. Along with their difference in colouring I knew from the first that they would never be mistaken for each other and I was glad that it wouldn't be easy for the world to pigeon-hole them as 'the twins.' A constant stream of friends and Church family trekked to the Hospital to visit us. When the Vicar came and prayed for us, the babies were miraculously silent, launching into lusty yells the moment he stopped!

Outside, the sun was shining, the grey days were over and I was beginning to feel pretty claustrophobic cooped up in my hospital room. I was desperate for fresh air, home food and my own bed. We left when the babies were five days old, still with a question mark over their feeding. Two days later my milk finally came in, along with floods of tears and a night when I thought I was sinking back into deep depression again, but which turned out to be merely the 'baby blues.' I tried feeding the girls myself all over again but it was such a juggling act that I needed at least two more arms to make it possible. No sooner did I get one latched on than the other one fell off and they both fed so slowly that there weren't enough hours in a day to feed one after the other. Kay still hadn't really got the hang of feeding from me anyway and I felt terribly guilty that she was getting so little of my milk. The situation made me miserable because I desperately wanted both babies to have the very best nutrition. In the end, I rang the NCT Breastfeeding Counsellor and she was wonderful. She arrived with an industrial-looking breast pump and although I felt slightly bovine when it was all attached, I was ready to grasp at anything that kept me breastfeeding and it did the job superbly. I began a regime of using the pump seven times a day for 15 minutes. The milk was then bottled and divided between the two babies so that they each had their fair share of it. If there wasn't enough, we topped up with organic formula milk. I fed and cuddled one of the babies while either Mum or Jeremy fed and cuddled the other and then at the next feed I swapped so that I had plenty of close time with both of my daughters. I still felt guilty that I couldn't perfectly breastfeed them both and sad that I had to share them at all during feeding, but it was the best I could do in the circumstances. The pump enabled me to express milk for eight and a half months and both babies would even still feed directly form the breast occasionally, which was lovely. We instituted a policy of always feeding the babies at the same time, even if we had to wake one to fit in with the other, as it was impossible to get enough sleep or leave the house otherwise.

Both babies were thriving and growing fast and as soon as the feeding was sorted out I began to recover quickly, too. During the first six weeks, which felt at least six years long, I remember wondering how on earth I was expected to return to full sanity while looking after two babies, sleeping for only a few hours a night and recovering from major abdominal surgery. I worried constantly that I wasn't giving the girls as much love as they deserved because I was still depressed. And yet, despite everything, I did get better. The body heals itself amazingly and the total change of circumstances aided my mental recovery. I dreaded sickness, boredom and isolation, but thrived on constant activity and society. Even my regular panic attacks were vanquished by the utter exhaustion of twin motherhood.

It wasn't just my perception of the world that had changed. Spring and summer 2002 really were lovely and though it took forever to struggle out of the house amidst the constant feeding, changing, expressing, washing and cooking we made the effort to get out into the sunshine for a walk each day, which improved my mood and often transformed the girls' moods for the better, too. My two sweet little babies generated an enormous amount of attention, which I loved! Getting to know them, taking them to Church for the first time, showing them off to family and friends and seeing those first lovely smiles gave me so many positive moments that I didn't have to make an effort to seek them out any more. There were, of course, moments of exhaustion, tears, confusion and general madness, when the house was in an uproar of screaming babies, nappy disasters occurred and no-one managed to find time to cook tea. One month after the birth, Jeremy and I tried to do our accounts to discover that our combined brainpower was insufficient to work out 10 plus 10! But on the whole I remember a huge amount of laughter because the pregnancy was over, I could now share the joyful burden of caring for the girls and my sense of humour, motivation and zest for life had finally returned.

Over the next few months, as I began to feel mentally stronger, Mum and Dad slowly backed off until we were all leading our own lives again, but now with a pleasant routine of involvement established between us. Mum helped with most of the feeds during weekdays until the girls were a year old, she came swimming with us, shopping with us and babysat on a Thursday night so that we could go to Scouts. Scouts was still very important to me because it provided me with a bit of my old life, somewhere I could be just myself for a while. By the time the girls were four months old the depression had completely lifted. Figuratively speaking I held my breath each day for weeks, unable to believe that I was really out of it, waiting in trepidation for a low mood to hit me. Gradually I accepted that it was over and that if I did occasionally feel a bit morose it was for more normal and natural reasons. I had lived through nine months of severe depression and survived and, surprisingly, felt much stronger and more confident because of it, equipped as I now was with far greater knowledge of myself and a range of techniques for coping with times of difficulty (and there were plenty of those looking after the girls). And I could finally turn to God in heartfelt prayer and thank Him, not just for my wonderful daughters but also for walking with me through the valley of the shadow of death and bringing me safely out on the other side.

Back in my right mind at last, my old ideas and hopes revived and I had important decisions to make.

5th July, 2002 *I've made my mind up not to go back to work as I simply couldn't bear to miss these precious early days of Hattie and Kay's lives. They are hard but wonderful work and I love their company so much.*

It is a decision I have never regretted. We tightened our belts accordingly, accepting that there would be no new cars or expensive holidays for a long time. I also renewed my determination to continue having a TV-less home (we hadn't had a TV for ten years by then), choosing to fill our time instead with a pleasant routine of walks, parks, reading, singing, swimming and social visits. We also began to take Hattie and Kay with us on Scouting activities, which proved challenging but possible with support from family and friends. Caroline and her husband kindly loaned us their trailer tent for Summer Camp in August, when the girls were 5 months old, and our long-suffering parents camped with us, splitting the week between them. The previous year I had missed camp altogether, so it meant a great deal to me to be there. Reaching each anniversary of my difficult year was upsetting, but also represented a stage in the process of recovery as I had the chance to replace dreadful memories with much happier ones. We had a fantastic week with the Scouts and the girls were just brilliant, sleeping well in the fresh air and watching the lads with total fascination! That week we discovered the benefits of extended family living as there was always someone on hand to entertain the girls or push them down the field to rock them to sleep.

The birth of Hattie and Kay wasn't the only miracle we celebrated that year. Helen, who had valiantly supported me through the early part of my pregnancy despite losing her own baby in an ectopic pregnancy many years before, and who hadn't conceived since that time, came to me with wonderful news in the sixth month of my pregnancy. She was also pregnant, after sixteen childless years of marriage and her beautiful daughter was born in August 2002, five months after my little girls. How we truly shared her joy and praised God for this wonderful and unexpected answer to prayer. As soon as camp finished, we plunged into organising Hattie and Kay's Christening. Along with some of our old friends, we asked Helen and Ali to be Godmothers to our girls because in my hour of need they both showed true Christian love to me and I couldn't think of any better examples for my growing girls to follow.

15th September 2002 The Christening was wonderful. Hattie and Kay looked gorgeous in the long white gowns I made for them! Church was packed out and the atmosphere of joy, love and worship was palpable. I took the chance to thank the whole Church for their loving support of Jeremy and I throughout my pregnancy and after. The whole thing was beautiful. So, my little ones begin their Christian journey. I hope and pray that they will always know Jesus as their Saviour.

My vision of 'I am pregnant' written on a particular page of my diary came true the day I was given the news of my positive pregnancy test, but what of the other visions? I don't remember the exact occasion on which the vision of me drying a baby after a bath came true, but there were plenty of times that fitted the bill. However, I can remember when the vision of me holding a baby over my shoulder while sitting in a rocking chair in our smallest bedroom came true. Mum and Dad bought me a rocking chair for my birthday two months after the girls were born; we stashed it temporarily in the smallest bedroom, which was just a store for baby stuff at that point. One evening a few months later, we had pursued our bedtime routine to great success with Hattie, who was fast asleep in her moses basket in our bedroom, but to no avail with Kay, who was grizzling. I didn't want her to wake Hattie up, but I also didn't want to take Kay back downstairs as that would have woken her up even more. In desperation, I sought a quiet place in the cluttered little bedroom. We sat together on the rocking chair and I phoned some friends for a chat in order to keep myself calm. I chatted and rocked and held Kay over my shoulder and eventually she fell asleep. And then something clicked into place. I had foreseen this moment and now it had come to pass. I only used the rocking chair there once as shortly afterwards we moved it out of that room. It was a clear confirmation that the visions were truly God's promises to me.

My diary shows a new Mum's delight and fascination at the development of her children. I wrote pages and pages about the girls and, once my depression was truly over, very little about anything else. I could watch them for hours, marvelling over their achievements, observing with great interest the very obvious differences in their characters and often feeling moved to tears by their beauty. That first year was a voyage of discovery into the fascinating subject of child development and the slightly less fascinating area of childhood illnesses and domestic disasters. I ricocheted between laughter, exhaustion and the occasional sense that it was all a bewildering and amazing dream. Could these beautiful babies *really* be mine? I had years of dreams and hopes to fulfil in the raising of these long-awaited children, so I threw myself into their care with a determination to make the most of every minute.

Some of those minutes were very trying, of course, and every day brought it's challenges. I simply didn't have enough hands to attend to the needs of two babies at once, so, as with feeding, I had to develop techniques to cope. One of them was the use of my voice instead of my arms as a means of calming and entertaining. I sang to the girls constantly so that I could keep one calm while feeding/changing/winding the other and I sang to entertain them both while I cooked or did other essential jobs. It was hard work having to sing all the time, but a lot less stressful than having two babies wailing at me. Learning nursery rhymes is good for children anyway, but I sang so much that it had an amusing and slightly bizarre consequence. For several of their early years the girls would burst into song (not necessarily the same one) as soon as they had finished eating, much to the amazement of friends and people at nearby tables in restaurants!

Taking two babies out and about was tricky. We coped by purchasing two single buggies and a second-hand double. That way one parent could take both babies out in the double but if two adults were on an outing we could switch to the two singles, which allowed us to get around much more easily. Nap time was another challenge. For eight months I ran myself ragged trying to cope with two babies who never slept at the same time during the day. I paced the streets with them for hours to keep them both happy so that the one who wanted to be awake could look around while the other was being rocked to sleep. Finally, I decided to impose a routine for all our sakes, but not one where I left them to cry alone. I couldn't rock them both in my arms or feed them to sleep, so I began to put the girls in their single pushchairs with a toy and a blanket when they were tired. Then I sang and rocked them until they dropped off. If one was still unsettled, I could park the sleeping baby and push the yelling one into a different room. Similarly, if one woke before the other, I could remove her without disturbing her sister. After a few weeks they accepted the routine and most days it worked. When they woke from their naps, sometimes grouchy, I would sit them on my knees (it was a several stage process to get them both there!) and read them touchy-feely books or stories until they were fully awake and ready to be active again. We read to them at least three times a day every day for their first few years and both of them quickly developed a pleasing love of books which grew naturally out of those times of peaceful togetherness.

On the whole looking after twins was incredibly hard work and I often felt that parents of singletons just didn't understand. I found it rather isolating when I couldn't physically manage the social activities that the singleton mothers chose. I particularly remember when we started going to toddler groups how I struggled because the girls each needed me to help them do something simultaneously, usually on opposite sides of the room, and I constantly felt torn and harrassed. Hardest of all, our nights were very disturbed indeed and we didn't have a full night's sleep for at least 18 months. I am glad that early on we joined the Twins and Multiple Birth Association (TAMBA) because their magazines were reassuringly full of parents of multiples having similar experiences.

Those were some of the challenges of having twins, but on the very positive side, the exciting milestones of first words, first steps and so on were all the more fascinating for having *two* children developing together, spurring each other on and interacting amusingly. From two months old, when we sat them on our knees facing each other and they grinned at each other with delight, the girls were great company for each other. At every stage they reached, every game they wanted to play, every story they enjoyed, they were accompanied by a sister liking all the same things at the same time. From very early on they shared (and still share) a wonderful imaginative world. When their language moved on to the stage of story-telling, which happened very early in our household, they began what a relative termed 'competitive story-telling,' where they spun a story rapidly and incessantly, wresting the narrative backwards and forwards between them. Some days they narrated everything they did! All I had to do to keep them occupied was read a story or make a suggestion and they were off, changing and adapting, making the story their own, demanding tea towels, wooden spoons, bowls and all sorts of other unlikely objects be put at their disposal for costumes and props.

Mothering twins required all my organisational skills and ingenuity, stamina and inventiveness, but it was easily the most satisfying work I had ever tackled and such a privilege to be allowed to nurture and shape two young lives. The girls grew and changed so fast that I was aware every day how incredibly precious the time I spent with them at home was.

9

We now had the family we had always wanted and were making the most of our new lives in every way we could, so in late 2004 I was taken aback by a growing sense that our family was incomplete. I was similarly puzzled by two visions that were still unfulfilled. One was of me walking on a path on the common with a toddler, but just *one* toddler, not two. I had never walked that way with only one of the girls, so I now began to wonder if the vision showed a different child. The other vision was of a toddler standing upright with arms outstretched to me at the end of its cot, but the cot was in our smallest bedroom in a place where Kay's cot had never stood and by then she was in a bed. Again, I had to conclude that the child in the vision must be a different one. Combined with my own growing sense of incompleteness, I felt that perhaps the remaining visions were a promise and an encouragement from God that there would be another child for us.

Jeremy and I talked it over. Since the last experience, we had both regularly protested that we never wanted to go through another pregnancy, but now we found that we both wanted another baby enough to overcome our fears. All over again I was hit by the longing to conceive naturally, without injections, drugs, scans and teams of medics and although I knew how unlikely it was, I wanted it very badly, desperately hoping that we wouldn't have to revisit the hospital for our stored embryos.

Although my prayers once again turned into pleas that God would fulfill His promise *my* way, I had recently begun to understand the good God could bring even from our darkest experiences and to realise why He might choose to journey with us through them rather than lifting us out of them, as we would have preferred.

21ˢᵗ July 2004 I've had several chances recently to give back a little of the love and support I received when I was in need. I have supported an old friend through ICSI. I don't think she even felt able to discuss what she and her husband were going through with her closest family, so I was glad to be able to help. Then another friend and his wife shared with us that they had recently lost a baby through miscarriage and we talked for ages, glad that they felt able to confide in us.

Over the next few years, a stream of people shared their stories with us, often expressing their relief at having the opportunity to talk to someone who genuinely understood their situation. Through them all, I came at last to the realisation that my own suffering had qualified me to give that support and I discovered that there is a joy in being truly useful to someone in need that I had never really experienced before. It was a joy that went so deep it washed away the bitterness and resentment left over from my own bad experiences. I no longer wondered 'why me?' Instead, as I looked around and saw into other people's lives, my thoughts became, 'why *not* me?'

But the pain of infertility was beginning to reawaken in me, too. A couple of years rolled by and my desire for a third child grew stronger. Although I longed desperately for a natural pregnancy, grasping eagerly at any story of infertile couples miraculously conceiving naturally (this happened to some friends of ours), eventually I had to face the fact all over again that it wasn't going to happen. By that point, Hattie and Kay had just turned four. It was time to think about returning to the Priory Hospital for help before the gap between our children became too big, time to decide whether we could cope with all of the trauma that it might bring. Jeremy was uncertain for a long time about the wisdom of this step, worried that I would end up depressed again. I was afraid, too, but a deep conviction drove me on. Finally, our decision was made.

5th April 2006 I rang the Priory Hospital and made an appointment to see the Consultant. I had some apprehensions, principally about stirring up painful memories from my days of depression, but underneath them I felt surprisingly calm in spirit. As we stepped through the door, I was suddenly struck by the thought that some important bits of our property were very close by – our 15 'spare' embryos in storage.

The Consultant was great. He agreed to a couple of tries with the frozen embryos on a natural cycle, as I cannot bear to be messed around by drugs again, and each time with just one embryo put back. It reduces our chances, I know, but I'm more interested in giving Jeremy and I and the girls a chance to cope with it all. We went away with the instruction to ring as soon as my period starts, if we're ready to go ahead. That could be as soon as next week! All that remains after years of contemplation of this subject is to pray that if God wants us to have another child that He will sustain us through it all as He did so faithfully before.

I'm back to weeing on sticks and using my Persona monitor. The first bit of the business is to work out when I'm ovulating so that we know when my womb would be ready for an embryo. Then we'll just pop one in. It sounds so easy…

I took the opportunity to buy a book about IVF designed specifically for IVF children to help me explain to Hattie and Kay what we were about to embark on (as they would have to come with me to the hospital occasionally) and to help them understand how they themselves came about. Rather than allow the idea to come as a shock to them when they were older, we felt it would be much better if they knew and accepted it from an early age. My main points to convey were that they are made up of the same basic material as everyone else and that they are some of the most wanted children on the planet! They took it all in their stride.

When my period started, I rang the hospital and was booked in for an initial scan to check that all was well and to begin tracking my natural cycle. I went again on Day 14 and the scan showed that I was nearing ovulation. The next job was to detect a hormone surge, so I was given a pack of Clear Blue sticks and told to ring in each day.

27ᵗʰ April 2006 The hormone surge which triggers ovulation is just beginning. Today the Nurse measured the thickness of my womb lining and said, "impressive endometrium, Rebecca!" I felt absurdly proud of my womb!! There will be another scan to check that I've ovulated, then Embryo Transfer on Bank Holiday Monday, if the embryos survive the thawing process.

I felt very calm at the outset, praying for God's will to be done and also supported in prayer from the outset by a couple of good friends. The next scan showed that I had successfully ovulated, the follicle had been released and I was pronounced ready for the next stage.

30ᵗʰ April, 2006 This morning two of our frozen embryos will be removed from the freezer. If they survive and are good, one will be implanted tomorrow. If not, another two will be removed, and so on, until we have a suitable one. I'm waiting for a phone call now to tell me what has happened and my hands are shaking as I write. Everything hinges on this. Will those embryos survive? If none of them do, that's it, our chance of another child is gone forever. I could never go through the process of embryo creation again. I've been so calm until now but nerves have really hit this morning. It's great that I still have to give the girls breakfast, dress them, etc., as it keeps me occupied. What will happen? When will the phone call come? I rang my prayer team first thing asking them to pray for us this morning. Will we make it to embryo transfer? I'll know soon. It's 9.45 a.m. The call should come before 11 a.m.

I sat next to the phone, shaking, waiting for the call, all sorts of scenarios playing through my mind. I was afraid of having no viable embryos and simultaneously afraid of having too many, as I didn't wish to waste any but still adamantly wanted only one implanted. It was a long couple of hours as I sat and waited.

30ᵗʰ April, 2006 (cont.) The call came from the department Manager at 11.30 a.m. I had to get her to repeat several times what she had to say to be sure I understood. They took 4 embryos out (I thought they said 2 on Saturday?). Two were at 2 p.n. stage (pro nucleii, just after the first cell division). Of these, one was damaged through not being dehydrated enough when it was frozen so it failed straight away and the other looks ok, so they'll keep watching it. The next two had been frozen at a later stage. Both have survived and one looks better than the other. If they don't make it through the night, they'll take out some more tomorrow and try again as we're still within the implantation window. I said I'd really rather we didn't have to take out any more as I only need one and we need to save the rest if it doesn't work. She said of course, but she's pretty confident we'll have something to implant tomorrow. We've to be there at 8 a.m.

Phew. I cried buckets when she rang off, partly as the tension of waiting was released and partly because it really hit me that it might not work. Oh why can't I just get pregnant like normal people? I'd assumed because the frozen Embryo Transfer went so well last time that it would again this time as a matter of course, but that isn't the case. Come on, little embryos, I only need one of you to be a go-er.

I'd also forgotten what an emotional rollercoaster this is. It takes me right back and it also makes me realise all over again how astonishingly blessed we are to have Hattie and Kay. My terrible pregnancy and depression obliterated all thoughts of that miraculous conception, but now I can appreciate all over again just what we achieved and against what odds.

2ⁿᵈ May 2006 I went to bed that night and had strange embryo-related dreams all night, frequently waking feeling slightly panicky. I was far more stressed than I realised. Yesterday morning we all got up at 6 a.m., were out of the house by 7 a.m. and all at the hospital by 8 a.m. A family Bank Holiday day out! One of the Embryologists came to see us and said that of the 2 p.n. embryos, one had survived and was a class 1 / 2. Of the second batch that were thawed, neither had progressed and so weren't viable. So only one out of the four was viable, but we had the one we needed and it was a relief not to waste any of them. Then Embryo Transfer went ahead. Jeremy and the girls waited in the waiting room. I'd forgotten how undignified it is lying on your back with your legs in stirrups and your whole bottom bared to the room. It was a bit uncomfortable and then I was allowed to dress, walk next door and lie down for 20 minutes, which was very relaxing. I prayed while the embryo was implanted and afterwards, too. It was all over by 9 a.m. Thank you, Lord, for this chance of another precious child. Now I just have to make it through till next Friday and the pregnancy test. I'm supposed to take it easy now, but how does that square with four year old twins?!!

I was back to looking for signs with a vengeance, constantly saying to Mum, "If only I could know what's going to happen."

"It's probably better that you don't," she usually replied.

At points I speculated wildly, while at others life felt so normal that I had to remind myself that anything was different. The usual routine was so helpful in getting through the days and though I wasn't able to rest much I didn't do anything strenuous. The girls were very understanding, not climbing on me and clambering into their car seats unaided for the first time. For the first week my tummy ached on and off. Then at the beginning of the next week, PMT seemed to hit, with the usual moods and tummy aches. When my breasts suddenly felt tingly and tender I began to feel hopeful despite the PMT, but at bedtime on the final night before the pregnancy test, nerves hit with a vengeance and I drifted in and out of confusing dreams about pregnancy tests and blood. By 6.30 a.m. I couldn't stand it any longer. I tiptoed to the bathroom, did the test and waited. It was negative. Shaking, I took it to show Jeremy and then we curled up together and held each other for a while without saying much. I was bitterly disappointed. After a while we chatted quietly and agreed that we would carry straight on with another cycle. The girls woke up, we got on with the day and I was fine until I spoke to Mum. She was so disappointed for me that it made me admit my own sadness and I cried when I came off the phone and for several rather desperate hours afterwards.

The experience left me feeling shaken and melancholy and very clingy towards Hattie and Kay, needing the reassurance of their presence in my life, which they gave just by being themselves. When I told the girls that the embryo hadn't been strong enough to become a baby, they took it matter-of-factly and Hattie said, "Now the embryo has gone, Mummy, you can run and run today." So we went to see the bluebells on Chase End Hill and I did.

As the days passed, I realised that despite the outcome and the stress, I had actually enjoyed the hopefulness of the twelve days of waiting because at least I had a real chance of a pregnancy during them. I decided to thank God for the fortnight of physical activity ahead of me before I turned my body over to the process of assisted procreation once more and to rest in the fact that His timing would be just right for me, despite the fact that the gap widened every day between the twins and a prospective sibling.

We still had nine frozen embryos left, so, feeling assured that there were enough to provide us with at least a couple more tries, we embarked straight away on the next cycle of treatment. I was primed and ready for the next Embryo Transfer, when we received the worst possible news.

1ˢᵗ June, 2006 Oh Lord, oh Lord, what a dreadful day yesterday was. They began to take the embryos out ready for Embryo Transfer today. I spent the morning painting the kitchen, keeping busy as I've been doing for the last fortnight. Then the phone rang and it was the Embryologist. And she said, "I have some bad news for you. We've taken all of the embryos out and they've all failed." Nine of them, all nine of them.

And I said, "What, all nine of them?" and she said yes and I was so stunned I couldn't work out what to say next. She explained that half way through she had swapped with the other Embryologist in case it was something she was getting wrong, but it kept on happening.

"They didn't like being frozen," she said. I collected myself and we chatted for a few minutes and that was it. Towards the end of the conversation I could feel something bubbling up inside and as soon as she rang off it came out as a long, painful wail. All our embryos gone in one day. Last month had been our only chance and it failed. Those embryos had stood for so long as our hope of more children, real chances where none had existed before.

I was grief-stricken. I'd been thinking for so long of our family as a lovely family of four, soon to be five. We took it into consideration when choosing a new car, we had planned how to move the girls bedrooms around to fit another child in, we carefully kept all our best baby gear in readiness. Staring at a totally changed mental landscape was a bleak experience and all the more shocking because it had changed so completely in one day. I felt a totally desperate urge to be with my girls, for them to prove to me that I *was* a mother, that I still had them. I remember going in to check on them before I went to bed that night and hanging over each of them for much longer than usual as they lay peacefully asleep, drawing immense comfort from their very existence.

1ˢᵗ June, 2006 (cont.) I was so full of despair that it took me ages to get to

74

sleep. Then just before I dropped off a new spark of hope seemed to lighten my heart. I realised what it was when I woke this morning. It had suddenly occurred to me that despite the sheer terror that it stirs in me, a fresh cycle of treatment is actually a possibility and that having a slight hope, even if we decide not to take it, is vastly better than having none at all. It's not all over yet.

I feel like I have suffered a bereavement. Life goes on but something has gone forever. The sense of bereavement regularly sweeps over me, knocking me off balance and leaving me casting around desperately for something positive to latch on to. I'm taken aback by just how much I wanted another child, enough even to contemplate full ICSI treatment again.

Over the next few days, my mind endlessly weighed possibilities, because I needed possibilities and not this dead-end. Jeremy and I discussed the situation and we came to the following conclusions. Neither of us could face accepting that we would never have another child, so we agreed that we both felt happier contemplating further treatment as a possibility. However, although the desperate part of me wanted to carry straight on, this seemed a very unwise course. We knew we would be better off making a decision about further treatment when our emotional state of loss had subsided. We knew a whole fresh cycle would be much harder on me mentally and physically, which is why we needed to be united and sure. So we made a plan to leave the final decision until the beginning of the following year. That way I could enjoy our last term together before Hattie and Kay began full-time school without feeling ill or stressed from treatment. I knew I would really regret it if that last 'home' term was spoilt by my fixation with having another child and I thought that Hattie and Kay deserved good quality attention from their Mummy while they were still allowed to be with me doing nice homely things. In the meantime, at least we could make some efforts yet again towards a natural conception. Our chances were probably half a percent of nothing but it was worth a try because if it happened it would solve the whole problem. We couldn't rule out a miracle either. Maybe this was after all the way God would fulfill His promise.

When I told the girls as matter-of-factly as possible about the embryos not surviving, their reaction surprised me. Kay was genuinely upset, her little mouth turning down at the corners. She started saying something in a tiny plaintive voice and when I knelt down and listened, she was saying, "But I don't want our family to be just what it was." She really wanted another child in our family. Hattie didn't say much until later. She'd obviously been thinking it over because at tea she suddenly asked,

"What happened to our embryos?"

I explained that they hadn't been strong enough to live. Later still, she came and asked,

"Mummy, were me and Kay strong embryos?"

I reassured her that yes, she and Kay were very strong. It made me wonder if perhaps we shouldn't have talked so much to them about a third child. Then again, they would have asked questions about all the hospital visits and at least it gave us the chance to discuss their own origins with them. Anyway, for a few months I was to have a rest from it all, so I tried to take a step back and leave it in the hands of God.

3rd June 2006 *I prayed all along, 'Your will be done, Lord,' so I cannot doubt that the loss of the precious embryos is part of the plan. Oh Lord, please give us your guidance and make it blatantly obvious so we can't be mistaken. Amen.*

10

So, we had a self-imposed thinking time of six months ahead of us. I felt at a total impasse, my longing for another child evenly matched by my fear of full ICSI treatment. Summer arrived and I prayed and prayed that God would make everything easy and bless us with a naturally conceived child. And then I prayed a bit less and a bit less until, months later, I had drifted totally out of touch with God, even doubting His existence. It was a horrible feeling. Then a sermon in Church based on Chapter 3 in Revelation, where the Church in Laodicea is accused of being lukewarm, shook me up as I realised that it applied completely to me. So I started praying again and this time I changed my prayer and instead of asking for a baby I began to ask that God would help me to right our relationship.

When I asked Jesus to be a part of my life again, everything began to change. One day I heard that quiet, authoritative voice telling me to invite one of my non-Christian friends on an Alpha Course. I was vaguely aware that an Alpha Course was about to begin at our sister Church, but had had no thoughts of attending myself. I nervously obeyed the prompt and to my surprise the friend agreed to come. In the end she attended for only a couple of weeks, but by that time I had become deeply involved with the other people on the course and knew that *I* needed to keep going. As with all of God's plans, it turned out to have amazing bonuses all round. I was able to support a friend who was being a group leader for the first time; I enjoyed the company of another friend from my NCT group who had also decided to attend the course; I was able to offer my own experience of Jesus to my group; and best of all for me, my own faith was reaffirmed.

It was an amazing course. One person who arrived with a display of outright hostility, shouting angrily at the startled Curate, calmly stood up towards the end of the course to inform us that he had decided to give his life to Jesus, describing just what a difference it had already made to him and his family. Others, too, had their lives transformed by a new understanding of God's love for them. By the end, I was buzzing with excitement and waiting expectantly to see what God would do in my life and the lives of those around me.

Open again to God's guidance, that is just what I began to receive. In Church one day as we sat quietly listening to what God had to say to us, I asked for a message for me about our family situation. There was a picture on the screen of a pair of feet standing in the sand. When the Vicar asked the congregation if anyone had a message to share, a lady from our Housegroup spoke up and said that she had initially thought the feet in the picture were standing still but had then had a strong sense that they had actually just taken a step forward, and that Jesus was saying, "Take that step forward, I am with you." I felt a little thrill in my heart and wondered if it was a message for me.

The next answer to prayer was quite unexpected!

18th November, 2006 I prayed desperately for a baby one night recently, waiting for my period to begin and the next day a job fell into my lap! Not quite the answer I wanted, admittedly, but the experience was so hot on the heels of my earnest prayer that I decided to go for it even though it seemed the opposite of everything I truly want. An NCT friend rang to tell me about it, I rang the employer and within hours I had the job! It's another admin. job but with more flexibility, less hours and better pay than my last. My new boss has even agreed that I can reduce my hours in the school holidays so it has no impact on the girls. The first day at work I felt sad that it might get in the way of my baby quest but I'm going to wait patiently to see what God will do with all this. I can see signs of His care in it. Some structure to my week will be good as I had been dreading losing the girls to full time school.

I was also very conscious of being a witness to my non-Christian new boss. How successful I was I will never know, but I know God was at work in his life because I have since heard that one of the difficult situations I prayed about for him has begun, against all expectation, to change for the better. Of course, the fertility situation was never far from my mind and I was still struggling with the way forward, when God gave me the clear, loving guidance I needed.

18th November, 2006 A few weeks ago while washing up and praying I had a sudden vision of Jesus weeping, His face contorted with sorrow and suffering and I had a sudden flash of revelation to accompany it. He shared in all of my sufferings and felt agonies of sympathy for me. My agony was His agony. And I felt He said to me, "I'm so sorry that IVF is the only way. I'm sorry that's the way it is for you." And I understood that it's horrid for Him to watch me suffer because He loves me so much. So now I know for sure that ICSI really is the only way. I'm still afraid, but coming closer to acceptance. I don't know why the Lord answers our prayers in this way when He could give us a different kind of miracle, but I think I can wait expectantly now, knowing that whatever happens, He can bring good out of any situation.

At the beginning of January, the girls started full-time school. I was so sad to lose my little companions and so afraid for them as they embarked on a new stage of their lives without me there to protect them. The night before they started I sat at the kitchen table and cried so much I had a sodden mound of tissues sitting before me. Then I pulled myself together and decided to concentrate on the wonderful times we've had and are still to have and how lucky I am to have any children at all. At the same time our six month break came to an end and we both knew it was time to ring the Priory Hospital again.

When it came to it, despite the clear guidance I had received, I was frankly too terrified to make the call. Instead I welcomed a distraction, which came in the form of some news about a new type of fertility treatment on offer in Oxford, IVM (In Vitro Maturation). It involves taking immature eggs from unstimulated ovaries and maturing them in the lab, followed by their fertilisation using ICSI. The crucial point for me was that there would be no need to stimulate my ovaries, and therefore no risk of Ovarian Hyperstimulation Syndrome. I was deeply afraid of the danger and discomfort of OHSS and had spent the intervening years wondering how much the incredibly high hormone levels in my body had been either directly or indirectly responsible for the depression. Hope flared in my heart that I would be able to side step the whole terrifying issue by pursuing a form of treatment in which I had to take far less fertility drugs. So I eagerly pursued the idea, only to be utterly frustrated.

22nd January, 2007 I just spoke to someone at the Oxford Fertility Unit and she said that they would only do IVM treatment on women with polycystic ovaries, despite the fact that it's a treatment that doesn't have the danger of OHSS and OHSS is much more dangerous than anything else. They won't even consider me. I'm crying so hard I can hardly see. I'm so scared of the treatment and yet I want the chance of another baby so badly. I was hopeful that IVM would be a less dangerous way for us. Now I need to examine my heart and see if I'm brave enough to go back to the Priory and try it all again.

[Later] Wow, Jesus, You are so amazing. Just after I prayed this morning I came across a story on the internet about the increased success rates of IVF in a group of women who were prayed for, which gave me such hope. And then who

79

should come unexpectedly to my door but Helen, the one person who really understands the whole issue. We sat at the kitchen table and talked it all through and prayed together and now I feel so much better.

My last hope of a different route gone, I couldn't evade the hard decision awaiting me any more. Bolstered by prayer, I finally made up my mind that I was ready to go through the treatment again, just once more through, right to the bitter end of all the frozen embryos that might result and that I would then never, never make myself go through it again. I was terrified.

26th January, 2007 Then I prayed, please Jesus if this is the right decision for our family, then let me experience Your peace and joy in my heart. The next morning when I woke up, I lay there with joy singing in my heart so strong that I was nearly laughing aloud with it! The sense of Jesus's love and care was intense and I knew that He would be with me through it all. So I rang the Priory Hospital a few minutes ago and we are to see the Consultant a week today at an unlikely time in the morning. I was shaking during the phone call, but I know it's right. Only God can give this peace in my heart in the midst of fear and anguish, so I will trust Him and step forward in faith.

The first thing to deal with was my fear that I would hyperstimulate again. I needed to convince the Consultant to let me have a very low dose of the fertility drugs, despite the fact that I was nearly six years older and that the previous time I had actually been on the lowest recommended dose. The Consultant was dubious about reducing the dose even more and insisted that I have a test to determine my hormone levels before starting. It meant a delay of another month, but it seemed vital to me to avoid hyperstimulation if possible. In the meantime, I thought over the unfulfilled visions and the more recent guidance I had received and tried to count on them as God's promises to me.

When the results of the FSH (Follicle Stimulating Hormone) blood test came, I was vindicated. The result was 6.6, which is apparently quite normal and proved that my age had made little difference to my hormone levels. As a consequence, the Consultant agreed to prescribe me a dose of Gonal-F that was one third lower than the usual lowest dose (100 iu as opposed to 150 iu). My fears subsided and I felt empowered by his concession. I knew so much more this time around and was determined to exercise greater control. I even began to experience little thrills of excitement that at last we were taking constructive action towards our baby dream.

*1ˢᵗ **March 2007** Spent last night surfing the internet trying to find information on mail order companies who could supply our drugs cheaper. I found a very helpful website called Fertility Friends which had pages of queries from members on exactly that subject, with answers from the experiences of other members. The prescription arrived today, a list of everything I will be injecting into myself.*

This is the prescription :
Inj. Buserelin
As directed 500ug daily s-c
three x 5.5 ml vials

Inj. Gonal-F Multidose
As directed 100 iu daily
12 days supply

Inj. hCG Pregnyl 10,000iu or Ovitrelle 250 ug
As directed
Amps.one

Supps. Cyclogest 400 mg
1 p.v. b.d. as directed
Supps. 32

Aside from this list of horrors, life is so busy. Planning for the girls fifth birthday party is taking up a lot of mental energy. They have asked for a Ball (!) and are very excited!!

We were funding ourselves completely, so every penny counted and focusing on the practicalities helped me to ignore my fear of what was to come. I felt experienced enough to make decisions this time about things like the form in which we would administer the drugs. I rang round some of the chemists recommended by people on the Fertility Friends website and was delighted when Applied Dispensary Services gave me a good quote of £278.70 for injector pens which sounded easier to use than the little vials Jeremy had had to mix by hand six years before. Another chemist I rang wanted to charge £505.92 for the same thing! Decision made! It really paid to do a little research. I posted off the prescription to them and then prayed that the drugs would arrive in time as I needed them within a week.

When they arrived it was time to head for the hospital for the appointment that signalled the beginning of the ICSI cycle.

9th March, 2007 *Busy morning as we went to see the girls swimming at school before heading off to the hospital. They looked so cute with their little yellow swimming hats and water wings on. Both did really well, especially considering Hattie wouldn't let go of the side last week!*

Then set off for Birmingham for the Day 21 appointment at 11.30 a.m. We took all the drugs with us in the polystyrene cool box they came in. Had to confess that I remember very little of the actual process from last time, so we had to be treated like novices. I wanted to learn how to inject myself this time, partly to be more in control, partly because I felt a bit braver this time and partly because if Jeremy has to go away for work I don't want to be in a panic wondering who will do my injections.

However, when faced with a half-inch-long needle and an instruction to stick it in my thigh, I began to shake. Every instinct was saying quite clearly, 'No! Do not stick that needle in your leg! It will hurt!' At which point the Nurse relented and gave me an auto-injector. She said they're trying to discourage women from using them, but it solved the problem nicely. My instincts were completely hoodwinked. It no longer involved sticking a needle in my leg, just pressing a button, and I was able to do the first injection.

We booked dates for my baseline scan and Egg Collection operation.

10th March, 2007 *I slightly muffed the first Buserelin injection at home. Had difficulty getting the drug into the needle with no air bubbles. Was all fingers and thumbs. The Nurse made it look so easy. Then forgot to squeeze a bit of it out to check there was no air in the needle. Then I was so tense I pressed the auto-injector really hard into my leg. Consequently, the injection hurt and my leg was sore for ages afterwards. Sigh. Will try to relax more tomorrow night.*

11th March, 2007 *Injection went much better tonight. Did it quietly in our bedroom, remembered everything and relaxed before pressing the button. It didn't hurt so much although it was still a little sore afterwards. I can feel a little lump under the skin where the drug was squeezed in. There is also a bruise where I did yesterday's injection.*

The previous two times I had taken the down-regulating drug, Buserelin, I had used a sniffer. This time it was injected and I was feeling very bold doing my own injections, but just as before, the effect was the same. Three days in and the hormones grabbed hold of me with a vengeance. The hot flushes were the least of my worries.

13th March, 2007 *Last night's injection ok. But today hormones hit. Called Jeremy a 'f****** a******' and nearly thumped him and that was before breakfast. Had just enough control to do it out of hearing and sight of the children.*

Stormed upstairs and calmed myself down. Not a good start to the day. It's obviously that day, the one on which I kicked the airing cupboard door during the first ICSI attempt six years ago. Ghastly.

Went down and apologised. Took a deep breath and tried to get on with breakfast but Jeremy was grumping about, which maddened me again. I was also suddenly very forgetful. Left Kay's cheese on toast under the grill until it burnt and Jeremy grabbed it. Left an egg boiling for 10 minutes, despite the fact that the timer went off after 4 minutes. I just didn't twig that I'd set it to remind myself that the egg was ready.

I tried not to say anything else to Jeremy at all and to get out of the house quickly. I was so glad to get the girls away from me and safely to school. Came home and threw myself into cleaning in an attempt to work through it. Met with my prayer support team. After school took the girls to Mum and Dad's. All was fine till Jeremy came home… then a wave of fury swept through me and I ended up storming out of the house and slamming the front door so hard that a pane of glass cracked. I walked round the block trying to school myself into silence so that I didn't return and say anything hurtful, but all I could see was a long dark tunnel ahead and suddenly I vividly recalled the feeling of sinking into a pool of depression… I so badly don't want to walk this route again and I honestly wondered whether we should quit now, while we're ahead.

I returned to the house to discover that Jeremy had been out looking for me. We tried to sit and eat tea together but I felt the intense anger returning so I took my tea on a tray and ate it in the study facing the wall as the wall didn't make me angry. Just the sight of Jeremy made me feel murderous. I never, never want to do this again. What a horrendous day.

And what a bizarre thing to sit there each night deliberately injecting myself with the very thing that warped my personality. Yet on I went. The Easter holidays loomed and we went away, taking the kit along in a special bag provided by the hospital and continuing the injections each night. Reporting in to the hospital for a baseline scan when we returned, I was told that my womb lining was thin and my ovaries inactive exactly as they should be, so we had a chat with the Nurse about the next stage. By then I was looking forward to the stimulating injections as I was fed up with my constant mood of irritable negativity. Jeremy was nervous, though, as he was to be responsible for injecting me in the bottom without the aid of an auto-injector. Instead he had to use a dial-a-dose pen with a long needle. I adminstered the Buserelin injection, struggling now to find an unbruised section of leg, and then Jeremy dialled 112.5 units of Gonal

F and did his bit. Despite the evil appearance of the needle, it hurt far less than the injections I was doing.

16th April, 2007 My mood has changed already, thank goodness. Jeremy said he could tell I was feeling more positive as I'm going around singing again. I feel like each day isn't a struggle now and suddenly everyone has stopped being irritating! I have begun a countdown of injections as both sets will end together. Last night it was three down, nine to go. I am also getting nervous as we approach the time when things will really begin to happen. But I am trying to rest in God's care and not worry.

19th April, 2007 On Tuesday I began to wonder whether the Gonal F was doing anything at all, but by Wednesday I felt a definite twinge in the tummy on both sides, and by this morning, Day 7 of stimulation, it was so strong it was uncomfortable to bend over. After taking the girls to school, Jeremy and I drove to the hospital for the scan which would usually take place on Day 8, but which has been brought forward at my insistence. By Day 8 last time I was in full hyperstimulation and I felt it would be better to know the situation sooner this time. Well, the scan revealed that I am hyperstimulating again, but not as badly as last time. Thank goodness I insisted on a lower dose! I have 15 measurable follicles on the right ovary, plus a few smaller. My left ovary was described as 'quiet' in comparison with 6 measurable follicles, plus a few smaller. The nurse thought it was too soon to reduce the dose of Gonal F as the follicles are still quite small, so she decided that I should continue with the 112.5 for two more days to develop them and then have another scan and probably a blood test to see how things are going. She also said that <u>all</u> my injections should be done into the bottom from now on as my legs are too bruised to continue using them. Poor Jeremy will have to do them all now!

I feel better prepared in all ways to tackle the stresses of ICSI this year and I continue to feel utterly convinced that this is just what we should be doing no matter what strange times are to come. I have lived through strange days before and come through with my faith and sanity both intact and by the Grace of God I shall again.

I sound very calm at this point, but I had only just taken my seat in the horribly familiar emotional rollercoaster. The ride itself was yet to begin.

11

Stress and anxiety hit me later that day, making it very hard to sleep. I worried about hyperstimulating and whether I would be ill and whether all the embryos would have to be frozen again and whether the high levels of hormones would have any effect on my mind. The next morning I took the girls to school and then returned home, sat in the sun by the patio doors and began to pray.

20ʰ April, 2007 Poured it all out to Jesus – how I'm very frightened, how I can't believe that I'm walking willingly back into my worst nightmares, how I hoodwinked myself into it by deliberately refusing to let myself think about how horrid it all was last time. And then, with tears dripping off my face, I thought about Jesus in the garden of Gethsemane. He knew what He had to face and He knew that it was worth it but He still experienced dread because what was to come was hideous. And though my situation in no way compares with the horror of what He had to go through, yet I know that we need to go through this and that it will be worth it in the end and that no matter how horrible things get God can turn it all to joy and good. But at this moment it just feels like suffering to me and it's comforting to know that Jesus knows all about it.

Strengthened, I pulled myself together and got on with the day, accompanied by my rounded, uncomfortable abdomen. Despite the hyperstimulation, the Nurse I spoke to later that day was reassuring. She seemed hopeful that we wouldn't have to freeze any embryos because they are more knowledgable now about how to 'coast' women in order to let the hormone levels settle and apparently very few women fail to make it to Embryo Transfer these days.

21ˢᵗ April, 2007 Scan went well today. The Nurse thought that although I have hyperstimulated it's well under control and everything should be fine. I have 13 follicles on my right ovary that are now over 1 cm and 6 on my left that are over 1 cm, so they all look very hopeful. There were also smaller follicles too numerous to count. The Nurse said it was pretty obvious that if I had had a higher dose in the first place, or continued at the same dose now, my ovaries would go haywire and I would be ill again. She decided that we should cut my dose to 75 units of Gonal F for the next two days and then review the situation at a scan on Monday morning. I didn't have to go for a blood test (hurrah! how I hate needles!) because she felt confident that my hormone levels weren't dangerous. Left the hospital feeling calm because the Nurse wasn't worried.

The staff managed the situation very well. On the lower dose over the next two days the ache in my tummy eased, but the follicles kept on growing. At the next scan, the Nurse found 18 measurable follicles on the right ovary and 8 on the left and recommended that I should have an Oestradiol blood test done to monitor me closely. The result was reasonably low, so the Nurse decided it was fine for me to have that day's 75u of Gonal F, followed by another scan the next day.

Driving repeatedly up and down the M5 to the hospital, I used the time to pray and poured out my heart to God, especially as the treatment became more stressful.

24ᵗʰ April, 2007 Dropped girls off at school and then sat in the car and uttered some very weary prayers for safety and strength and the Holy Spirit within me. Then set off for the hospital. Today's news is that the follicles are ready. Today I'll have my last injections and then that's it, time for the Egg Collection operation. Talked it all through with the Nurse. We have to inject the Buserelin at 6 p.m. instead of 10 p.m., then the Gonal F straight after. Then at 7.15 p.m. we inject the Ovitrelle which is supposed to ripen the eggs ready for the operation. Nothing tomorrow at all, but on Thursday we have to be at the hospital for 6.30 a.m., which means getting up at about 5 a.m. I will have been fasting from the night before, so the sooner it's over the better. Felt calm through the chat and relieved that we're nearly there now.

When I got back to the car however, I realised I was feeling very tense and on edge and I gave in and sobbed my heart out. Pulled out of my pocket my bit of rope that we were given in Church some weeks ago after a sermon about coping with problems. The rope represents the fact that we don't have to cope with our problems alone – the three interwoven strands are ourselves, the problem we are wrestling with, and Jesus who is helping us through it all. I'd been saving my rope because I knew that there were hard times ahead and it might help to have something to remind me that I'm not in it alone.

Anyway, I sat in the car and sobbed my heart out clutching my rope. Told Jesus how I felt it was so unfair that we had to conceive our children at a hospital with a cast of medics to help us instead of in the intimate embrace of a husband and wife. It's not fair. Why should we have to suffer this when most of the rest of the world conceives with the utmost ease and often not even intentionally. I sobbed out my terror that we might have gone through all this for nothing – weeks of injections, ups and downs, journeys to the hospital, hopes and fears, sleepless nights, and endless prayers – which could all crash into nothing if the embryos fail again, or if we don't even manage to produce any. Wringing the rope, I wailed like a frightened child because I don't want to have a general anaesthetic on Thursday morning and wake up in pain and then live with more anxiety and uncertainty for weeks. I don't want it to be like this. I wish it wasn't. I wish it wasn't.

When I came to the end of it all I held on tight to my bit of rope and closed my eyes and thought about Jesus. I thought about Gethsemane again and felt how cowardly I was in comparison and yet how He understands that this is hard for me, wimp as I am. The more I thought about Jesus the more I felt my spirits rising.

Then I dried my eyes and set off home, when suddenly I felt something welling up inside me, a massive burst of such intense joy that it was hard not to wind the window down and shout out how much God loves everyone! By the time I reached the motorway, I was laughing aloud, struck by the sense that with Jesus life is a big adventure and that (this is what made me really laugh) as the heroine of this particular adventure, it doesn't actually matter whether I succeed or fail because Jesus is the real hero and He has already won! What a cool adventure – all of the excitement and none of the real danger! The only real danger is of being separated from God and because of Jesus it just can't happen! Hurrah! I felt so happy I beamed at everyone I passed.

It just goes to show that even a demoralised and lacklustre request for the Holy Spirit is honoured by God with abundance. Like King David's experience thousands of years before, my cup was filled to overflowing. And I was reminded again that God blesses us with His Spirit not just for our own good but also for the good of everyone around us. As I gazed on the faces of the total strangers I passed I had such a strong sense of God's love and value for *them* as well as for me. It was like having a little peek at people through God's eyes instead of my own, sweeping away the suspicions and hostilities that cloud my vision and replacing them with the clear loving gaze of His.

With Egg Collection impending, I felt it was time to resolve the stressful question of exactly how many embryos to transfer back into my womb afterwards. We were still inclined to go for one, but we needed more information about how that would affect our chances. I requested a chat with the Consultant and he rang later that day. He informed me that of the 30% who achieve a pregnancy with two embryos transferred, 40% are pregnant with twins. He went on to inform me that transferring just one embryo reduced our chances from 30% to around 20%, although perhaps a little higher for those who have been successful before. He settled at a 25% chance if we went for one. However, as there wasn't much experience of transferring single embryos in the UK, he had little experience to share. He told me that in Sweden, where the Government pay for IVF entirely, most couples are actually recommended to go through their embryos one at a time because they realised that the cost to the State of a woman having twins was far greater than the cost of funding extra cycles of IVF. How long-sighted of them, I thought. In this country, where most couples fund their own IVF treatment, it simply isn't cost-effective because of the reduced chances, so two embryos is still the norm.

When Jeremy and I discussed the information later, we came to the conclusion that it would be better to spend £10,000 working through our embryos one at a time than to risk another set of twins and a cost of raising the extra child in the region of £180,000!!! But our final decision was only partly driven by finances. We simply wished to avoid the suffering it would cause me to go through another twin pregnancy, the real risk to the babies and the unbelievable impact it would have on our family. There was no point following our dreams of another child to the detriment of the lovely children we already had. So we prayerfully settled on one embryo, hoping that we would even get that far.

27th April, 2007 The operation is over now and I've survived! The day before the op. was fine. It was lovely to have a day with no scans or drugs. I went to work and really enjoyed doing something normal.

At 9 p.m. that evening we performed a house swap with Mum and Dad so that we would disrupt Hattie and Kay as little as possible. The next morning, we were up at 4.45 a.m. and off at 5.30 a.m., with my tummy hungrily rumbling. Arrived at 6.30 a.m. and checked in, then we were shown to a nice private room. The preliminaries over, we were both taken up to the fertility centre where we met the Consultant and the Anaesthetist. I always find it a bit alarming when I have to meet medical professionals who are about to do painful things to me!!

Kissed Jeremy goodbye (he was off to do his bit) and went into the little theatre. Was very nervous by this point, but the staff were very kind. Had a needle put in the back of my hand, which I loathe, for the anaesthetic to be administered. Then I lay and prayed until I felt a coldness spread up my arm and over my head and everything went blank.

I began to come round as I was wheeled back to the private room where Jeremy waited. I vaguely registered someone say that they had collected 18 eggs, but it took me a long time to be conscious enough to take it in. I didn't want to come back out of the restful darkness because my abdomen was painful, but it was worth it to have achieved 18 eggs!! I felt jubilant! At last we were back to the situation of a few years ago, with lots of potential children 'in the bank', a truly lovely feeling for an infertile couple. All those possibilities where none at all existed before! I was so glad.

The Consultant popped in and said that "18 was an excellent crop," which made me laugh. The pain receded gradually and then we had a visit from the fertility Nurse, who said that the Embryologist would ring tomorrow with an update on how many had fertilised. The Embryologist was injecting the sperm into them all as we spoke.

We were free to go. I walked slowly and rather achingly back to the car feeling thoroughly contented with my morning's work and not even anxious about what news we would get tomorrow. Surely we would end up with a couple of embryos out of that lot, I reasoned. Besides, God was in charge and I was happy to wait and see His plans for us unfold. We collapsed into bed when we arrived home.

I spent ages reading to Hattie and Kay, enjoying their cheerful company. My tummy is still uncomfortable and quite distended now, but I'm definitely not as poorly as last time. I am now using progesterone pessaries (called Cyclogest). They upset my stomach a bit.

The first bit of the waiting began. I went to work the next day, keeping my mobile to hand to receive the promised call from the Embryologist. Shortly after nine, she rang with excellent news. All 18 eggs had fertilised and were doing well! We had 18 embryos! All I could do was laugh - a 100% fertilisation rate and more embryos than we had ever had before! I immediately conveyed the news to Jeremy and Mum and Dad, all the time laughing with glee and a sense of the utterly surreal! I couldn't wait to tell my prayer team!

Meanwhile, the Embryologist was giving thought to what to do with them all.

27ʰ April, 2007 The Embryologist told me that the eleven that failed last year were late frozen embryos, whereas Hattie and Kay came from an early frozen (2 p.n.) batch. Therefore, she thought it would be wise to freeze a large batch today at the early stage. We agreed that she would freeze 12 and keep 6 out for the time being. She will ring tomorrow with an update and hopefully book me in for the transfer, although they will have to assess whether I'm well enough. I am still bloated but really feel much better than last time.

Wow! Thanks, Lord! We really have a chance of a pregnancy now. I know that a large number of embryos is no guarantee of success – look at what happened last year – but it is so lovely to be full of hope again.

The next day we had a call from the Embryologist to say that the six unfrozen embryos were doing well and that all had divided. Four were class 1 / 2 and two were class 2. Embryo transfer was booked for 8 a.m. the next morning providing the Consultant considered me well enough. My ovaries were so tender that I couldn't lean against anything, but I was so much better than last time that I felt very hopeful the transfer would go ahead. Another early start loomed, so the girls chose to go over to Mum's for the night. Having refused to think too far ahead, a new set of nerves now attacked me.

28th April, 2007 As we approach the distinct possibility of a pregnancy I am beginning to remember what it was like to be pregnant last time and wondering if I can really cope mentally with the sickness/tiredness/strange hormonal swings. Please help me, Lord.

That night I got down on my knees and prayed that God would make the one embryo He wanted the Embryologist to choose for us so much better than the others that her decision would be clear.

29th April, 2007 Up early and off to the hospital. The Embryologist met us with more good news. All of the six were still doing well, but one of them was doing particularly well and was now a class 1, so that would be the one we would have transferred!!! It was all easy and obvious. What an answer to prayer!

Went into the theatre and had to lie on the high bed and bare my bottom to the world. Really getting quite used to this now! The Consultant prodded my tummy about (very uncomfortable) and declared me well enough to proceed while cautioning me to ring immediately if I felt worse. The Consultant, Nurse and Embryologist were present and all were very cheerful and had me laughing. Jeremy sat on a chair in the corner. The transfer took place and I felt calm and glad. Then had to walk into the next room and lay down and rest for a while. A couple went in for their Embryo Transfer before us and another one went in after, so I said prayers for them, too.

I felt so glad to have made it this far and also to have a go with a fresh embryo, which we have never had before. I'm rather nervous of what the future holds, but it was lovely to relax and enjoy what we have achieved today.

Then we made an appointment for the pregnancy test on May 10th (11 days time) and left. Felt weary and hungry so Jeremy found us a restaurant and bought me a huge breakfast. Went to bed again in the afternoon while Jeremy took the girls in the garden. I felt very sleepy and content lying there, praying over my embryo and thinking silly things like, 'Come to Mummy, you little darling.

There's a whole family here who really want you.' Later on I e-mailed all my prayer team with heartfelt thanks and requests for a few more prayers!
With a healthy, never-frozen embryo on board for the first time, the long wait began yet again.

12

As we survived each stage of the treatment and prepared ourselves for the next, there was a bit of breathing space and reflecting time, a pleasure in the simple fact of having made it that far.

2nd **May, 2007** *My tum is still distended, but it reduces a little each day. The first few days after the operation I had to walk around pretty slowly as my stomach felt so uncomfortable. Now I can manage a more normal pace, although if I try to dash it still feels bad and is a reminder to slow down. I have also felt so tired, which isn't a bad thing. It makes me feel inclined to take things easy, which is exactly the right thing for the embryo. Last year I was in a quite different psychological state after Embryo Transfer, as if someone had put me in chains and all I wanted to do was shrug them off and tear around as usual. I was devastated when I didn't get pregnant then, but also a little relieved to be able to get on with life as normal. I think I had only just begun to get a little time back to myself after having the girls full time at home and was also still wary of having to take it easy because it reminded me too much of how trapped I felt when I was pregnant and depressed. This year I am so much more relaxed.*

Every time I imagine finding that I am not pregnant, my stomach turns over with anxiety, so it is better not to think about it. What I am concentrating on is living in the present. The fact is, I am really happy <u>now</u>. I have a good embryo in my womb, a class 1, the best we could possibly hope for. There is a solid chance I could be pregnant after so long of no chance at all, which is really comforting and exciting. I have survived the dreaded treatment and in doing so have faced and exorcised a lot of my fears. Yes, it was horrible, but it wasn't the huge ghastly nightmare it had become in my mind over the last six years. My little bit of suffering has resulted in 18 embryos. Once again we have a nice big barrier between ourselves and the gaping hole of infertility. We have Hattie and Kay to prevent us from ever being a childless couple again. This is a good position to be in and today I feel really happy because of it.

But fertility treatment isn't called an emotional rollercoaster for nothing. Embryo Transfer was the pinnacle of the upward stretch. I balanced for a lovely while at the top and then the downward rush began.

3rd **May, 2007** *Not quite so contented today. My mind keeps on going over the fact that we hardly have any chance that this will work. I can't bear the* *thought that I will find next week that I am not pregnant and then have to endure a period, with the constant reminder of our failure that it brings. I know it is silly to anticipate what might not happen, but I am feeling a bit down today. On a more positive note, I got back into some of my larger-waisted trousers today, so my tum is obviously shrinking.*

The tension became worse with each passing day and each physical symptom brought a constant reminder of my situation.

*4ᵗʰ **May, 2007** There is so much hope, blood, sweat, pain and tears resting on this. Absolutely doom-filled yesterday when I felt lots of period pain-type aches, which I often get a week or so before my period is due. Today I've had aches again plus quite a bit of breast tenderness, but obviously I don't know what to make of it all since these are symptoms of PMT, too. Jeremy assures me that when I was pregnant before I also had the period pains. All a bit inconclusive really, so I guess there's nothing for it but to wait.*

Really, really tired out by anything at the moment. I guess I'm still recovering from the bashing I've given my body over the last seven weeks. Still, at least the week has gone really quickly and the girls have been lovely. Today Kay gave me a scrap of paper she'd written on at school which said 'To Mummy, I hope you have a baby.' Actually, it really said, 'To Mummy I hope you have a daddy,' but I knew what she meant! She keeps stroking my tummy hopefully. Had a good prayer time this morning which restored my spirits a lot. Would really rather like my will to be done at the moment, but God knows that and will act for the best anyway, whatever that is.

My dread of discovering that we hadn't achieved a pregnancy intensified, particularly because I experienced so much tummy pain during the next few days. Two nights in a row I was actually woken up by it. The second time was the worst. It felt as if something was squeezing my womb area unmercifully. It went off after about 10 minutes, during which Jeremy provided me with paracetomol and a hot water bottle, but it was very frightening at the time. The next day I rang the hospital to seek advice. The Nurse seemed to think that it was quite normal, helpfully informing me that it was either a sign of pregnancy or menstruation, and told me I could safely take paracetomol for it.

*7ᵗʰ **May, 2007** Didn't go to church yesterday morning because of disturbed sleep and tummy pain. Also couldn't face all the friendly enquiries when in that gloomy mood. How can I be pregnant after all these gripes and aches? Has it all been for nothing? I'm desperate to know the truth and yet also not. I only want good news, not bad. Come on, little embryo, please still be alive. Jesus, please* *breathe your life force upon it, I beg you.*

Meanwhile, the couple who had shared their troubles with us after a work do some time ago had also been enduring their own IVF saga. I rang Diana to let her know how things were progressing for us and also to see how they were doing. I discovered that after three failed attempts, they were part way through implantation on a natural cycle. It did me good to think about someone else for a while and I promised to pray for her and ask my prayer team to pray for her, too. The long days crept on.

8th May, 2007 Bizarrely, it seems to be getting harder to wait and see the closer we get to the actual day of the pregnancy test. Last week I was contented to have a fresh Class 1 embryo on board, which was exactly what I'd most hoped for. This week I've had so much tummy pain that it's all been in my mind a lot more and I've been through a range of emotions, mainly gloom at the prospect of finding myself not pregnant. I'm trying to cheer myself up with the thought that if I bleed and then ovulate, I might be able to have another embryo transferred in only a few weeks time. My heart quails within me at the thought of having to go through this over and over, each time feeling a little more desperate. Jeremy just says philosophically, well, we'll just have to wait and see and there's no point speculating. He's right, but I confess it is getting increasingly difficult to keep my mind focused on anything else. I'm desperate to know if the test is positive. I do not wish to know at all if it's negative as then I will have to face cartloads of anguish. I'm trying to trust patiently in the Lord but it's actually proving rather hard in the face of my growing anxiety.

I asked my wonderful prayer team to pray for strength for me and our prayers were answered when I suddenly experienced another change of mood.

9th May, 2007 Suddenly cheered up a bit today. After the last few days dreading the outcome of the pregnancy test, I suddenly felt today that I could cope with it either way and that I was ready to face up to it. It's time to find out so I can adjust my mental landscape and face the future. I felt able to pray for God's will to be done again, although would still prefer mine, obviously. I still have lots of tummy pain, but no bleeding, so that's good. Got to the stage where I'm a bit afraid to look every time I go to the loo in case there is blood, but so far no sign of any. I'm still carefully squashing any hopeful thoughts that I might be pregnant in order to prepare myself. The more hopeful I let myself get, the further there is for me to crash down when I'm not.

Then the final day of the long wait was over and it was time to return to the hospital. I slept surprisingly well, rose in the morning and did my sample in the little pot provided. Jeremy and I took the girls to school together and then it was time to go and face the truth, whether I wanted to know it or not. One of my prayer team rang just before we left to say she would be praying for me, which made me feel a bit braver. At the hospital I handed over the sample pot and then we just had to sit and wait. It was the longest five minutes ever and the waiting room became more and more full of couples. I kept my eyes on the floor, heart pounding and stomach full of butterflies, praying desperately for the strength to endure.

10th May, 2007 Then the Nurse called us and we followed her to a small consultation room, where she declared as soon as the door was shut that the test was positive!!!!!!!!!!!!!! I had to ask her to repeat what she'd said and then I sat in one of the chairs and sobbed. All I could say was 'Thank God, thank God, thank God,' and hold wads of tissues over my eyes to mop up the tears. Jeremy and even the Nurse were teary, too. I'm sobbing again as I write this because thinking about that moment fills me with such a depth of emotion. I was teetering on the edge of a pit of despair and the Lord rescued me from it. After so long of hoping and longing and praying and last year's terrible moments of loss and my doubts and the suspense of the last two weeks, that in that one moment He should wipe it all away and replace it with such relief and hope and joy was too much to take in. Oh thank you Lord, for answering my prayers.

Then I tried to listen while she told me practical things about continuing with the pessaries till 12 weeks, etc. Just couldn't believe that we were talking the language of pregnancy about me. She asked me if I had started to swell up again and I suddenly realised that yes, I had. My trousers had started to feel tight again. The Nurse explained that my bruised and swollen ovaries are now being called on to produce hormones to sustain the pregnancy and it's making them more swollen than ever. I have to call if it's gets really bad.

We went to the reception to make an appointment for a seven week scan and all the Nurses were saying to me, 'Well done, Rebecca. Good decision to have only one put back!' And I thought, oh yes, it was, wasn't it, because I can enjoy the next few weeks unspoilt by the worry of whether I am carrying one or two babies.

We went back to the car holding hands and feeling full of wonder. I finally allowed myself to accept that the breast tenderness, tummy pains and tiredness had all been pregnancy symptoms after all. Phoned Mum straight away and she burst into tears. She said she'd been counting the minutes till I could possibly ring.

The people I was most anxious to tell were Hattie and Kay, but we had to wait a while for that, so I rang my prayer team and Jeremy spoke to his parents. Then it was time to go and collect the girls and for normal life to resume!

I managed to wait until they were installed in the back of the car before telling them that Mummy and Daddy had some exciting family news. We told them that Mummy was pregnant because the embryo was a strong one just like them and that it was doing well and that if it continued to do well it would become a baby. Both were so excited. All in a big rush Kay said, "I will help you feed the baby and cook so you don't have to, and cuddle it ..." and simultaneously Hattie said "I will share all my toys with the baby and we will be very good and not fight any more ..." Could hardly get another word in, but was very delighted that they were so pleased. I think they both thought the baby would be along in a few days time. They couldn't really fathom having to wait nine months!

I didn't have long to digest the fact of my pregnancy before everyone around us knew. Our two five years olds spread the news quickly!

11th May, 2007 Hilarious day as I realised that five year olds can't keep secrets, especially ones they're very excited about. Kay ran off across the playground calling "Bye Mummy, give my love to the baby!" At collection time I was cornered by the Headmistress, who asked me if there was some good news in our family. The girls have told most of the staff that there's a baby in Mummy's tummy. I can't hide it at the moment anyway because I am swelling up hugely and look four months pregnant already. It's fluid retention and bruising I think, but is rather uncomfortable and noticeable. Thank goodness it's been raining all week and I can go out in a coat! What a peculiar situation.

Floating along, buoyed up by delight and amazement at the wonderful turn events had taken, I hadn't forgotten that Diana was still struggling through her treatment. I rang her that evening as I knew that holding off would only hurt her more, desperately hoping that my news would give her more hope than pain. She was very excited for me and then explained her own situation. At her scan they discovered that her womb lining was thickening better on a natural cycle than it had ever done with drugs and that she was heading for a frozen Embryo Transfer at the end of the weekend!! I told her I would continue to pray for her and I got straight to it as soon as I came off the phone, thanking God for her chance of a pregnancy and asking that this time it would work for her, too. I couldn't bear the thought that my pregnancy might add to her pain if her treatment failed. It felt so important to me that Diana should have this joy, too, that I thought about her and prayed for her a great deal over the following days. And the news was good - that weekend three of their embryos survived the thaw process and she asked if we could pray for the decision about which ones to transfer.

14th May, 2007 *Good news again from Diana. By this morning one of the embryos had stopped dividing, but the other two were good and were both transferred first thing this morning. She was so excited to have a chance and was just settling into the long wait.*

Meanwhile, I needed to survive the early weeks of my pregnancy. My abdomen ached constantly and one morning I woke up with a terrible pain around my right ovary. It left me feeling pale and shaky, but it wasn't repeated. I was desperately eager to get to the 7-week scan to see with my own eyes that the embryo was developing normally. I engaged in regular conversations with Diana, whose mind was alive with speculation, needing to hear about my exact symptoms during the long wait in order to compare them to her own. We were so keen to be pregnant and have our children together that I felt almost as anxious for her as I had been for myself!

28th May, 2007 *I spent the day wondering about Diana and then discovered an e-mail from her on my return home. She did an early pregnancy test and is pregnant!!!!!!!!!!!! Such fantastic news! I cannot begin to express my wonder at what the Lord has done for us.*

Once again the timing of my pregnancy seemed significant. The last time, Helen and I had shared our miraculous pregnancies, each praising God for a chance we thought would never come our way. Now this time around I could share and celebrate with Diana! Although I had struggled with impatience so much over the years, I thanked God at last for His perfect, wonderful timing.

13

There were many milestones yet to pass which held a terror for me because of the traumas of the first pregnancy, but as the weeks passed I experienced each in a form so much milder than before that I was able to greet them with joy! The one I dreaded most was nausea. I was anxious when it began at 6 weeks just as before but I soon discovered that it wasn't nearly as severe this time around. I was never actually sick and my appetite remained. It made all the difference to me, the difference between laying on a sofa too ill to move and being able to carry on as normal; between finding every meal a hideous trial and being able to enjoy food. I was so glad that I hadn't let my fear of sickness put me off. This time it really was just a reminder that all was well. At seven weeks, the hospital confirmed this when we returned for the scan. The whole family witnessed the wonder of a flickering hearbeat in the tiny blob on the screen.

After that I was handed over to the NHS and could then have the pessaries which I used until 12 weeks prescribed by my Doctor, which worked out much cheaper. I was very excited to make my first appointment with the Midwife. And that was it, we were all finished with the Priory Hospital. Well, perhaps not quite finished, as once more we left behind 17 hard-earned embryos in a freezer.

Despite extreme tiredness, the pregnancy was so much easier on me that it gave me a chance to review what had happened before, accept it and forgive myself. It was an incredibly healing process.

11ᵗʰ June, 2007 *It's just so different from last time, I can't believe it. This must be what a normal pregnancy is like and I'm actually enjoying it. It's what I so longed to do. I had come to the conclusion over the last few years that I had made an appalling fuss at the beginning of my last pregnancy, but now I realise just how horribly ill I really was. It's a relief to stop blaming myself for not being stoic enough and to accept that that's how it was and also to realise that it is possible to have this experience without it being so terrifying. I feel like I am loosening the grip of a whole set of fears that have pursued me for the last five years.*

With two children already, life remained so busy that I had little time to worry about the baby. Meanwhile, Diana was having a difficult time, experiencing a bleed at 6½ weeks that terrified her.

28ᵗʰ June, 2007 The Priory gave her a scan and the baby was fine, heartbeat there (and just one), but Diana was terrified after all her miscarriages. Eventually Worcestershire Royal Hospital scanned her again at 7 weeks to set her mind at rest, although she was utterly convinced that the baby had died because her symptoms had changed and reduced a lot. When I heard, I put her straight on the Church prayer chain and got down on my knees myself. Felt a great sense of reassurance from my prayer. Anyway, the scan showed that the baby was still doing fine despite all her fears and the Priory offered to scan her at 8 and 10 weeks, with Worcestershire Royal Hospital to scan her at 12, so hopefully they will be able to help her through it all. It's completely understandable that she is scared after her bad experiences. I'm so hopeful that this time God will make it possible for her to carry the baby to term and that one day she will hold her own child in her arms for the first time. It makes me want to cry just thinking about it.

There was nothing for her to do but wait and hope. For us, the summer holidays began and we decided to go ahead with a camping holiday on the South coast. It was great and we could have stayed on for another day or so, but towards the end of the week I was pretty exhausted and wanted to be back at home. It was then that we had an unexpected adventure. We had been quite out of touch with Malvern and hadn't realised how much rain they had had during the preceding week, so our decision to go was taken, rather unwisely as it turned out, on local conditions only. As we drove north, we began to meet flash floods, sometimes bad enough to make us alter our route, but we assumed that once we made it onto the motorway we would be fine. Then we ran into huge traffic queues and switched the radio on to discover that the flooding was very bad indeed. We were trapped on the motorway until 3 a.m. (pretty dreadful with two five year olds in the car) and when we finally made it off we were met with the news that all ways into Malvern were impassable!

We spent what was left of the night in our trailer tent in a car park and woke to the news that there was no safe way across the River Severn in the whole area. Suddenly we were refugees! We decided to head for Jeremy's parents in Leicestershire, where we stayed until the floods receded. It was such a relief to get there. I was worried about the effect on the baby of all the anxiety we had experienced, but as I sank into a proper bed for the first time in a week, I felt it moving for the first time, at only 14 weeks of pregnancy. That little butterfly touch gave the best possible reassurance and I prayed with thanksgiving that God had kept *all* of us safe.

The other events of the summer were all very tame in comparison! I managed to go to Scout Camp, where being pregnant gave me a good excuse to go to bed early with the new Harry Potter book. Diana survived the early anxious stages of her pregnancy and I felt blessed in every way not only to be able to enjoy another pregnancy of my own but also to see a friend have her prayers answered, too. In September, Hattie and Kay moved happily into Year One and also passed another milestone when they started Rainbows.

My next task was to break the news of my pregnancy to my boss. My unexpected job had been incredibly useful in providing us with extra income and I could see now that the delay in achieving a pregnancy had actually left us in a much better financial position. By working I had entitled myself to a maternity allowance which really helped ease us into having me full time at home again. It was yet another reason to rejoice in God's timing. Perhaps, I reflected, the nearly six-year age gap between our children, which still caused me concern, would also prove to be another of God's blessing.

Autumn passed by as I drifted along in a happy state of pregnancy. It was now time to face a scary battle that I had shelved in a dusty corner of my mind over how exactly I would give birth. I was desperate to give birth naturally because in all honesty I had come to feel sadly cheated of the natural experience the first time around. With this aim in mind, Jeremy and I signed up for another NCT course, again run by the teacher who had helpfully shared her twin experiences with us before. Six years before, I hadn't really absorbed her information on the birthing process as I knew I was headed for a Caesarean. This time, I wanted us both to be well-informed so that we could take back control of the experience for ourselves.

We were delighted that Diana and her husband signed up for the same course. Then, before it concluded, Diana went into premature labour and gave birth to her son at just 33 weeks. Thankfully, despite his early arrival, he weighed in at a healthy 6 lbs and after the initial trauma of coping with him in an incubator, Diana and her husband were able to take their little boy home to begin life as parents. We were thrilled for them and delighted when they asked Jeremy and I to be Godparents to their son.

With friends new and old giving birth around me, I weighed my options more urgently, discussing my chances of a natural birth with my midwife, NCT teacher and the hospital Consultant. I had the impression that my greatest danger was of my Caesarean scar splitting, but I discovered that this was actually very unlikely indeed. The hospital information sheet put the chances at only 35 in 10,000 and it went on to inform me that there was a 12 in 10,000 chance that it would split during a repeat Caesarean anyway. With my mind at rest on that score, I began to make enquiries about having my baby at home. I had been through so many unnatural experiences in recent years that I had a dread of hospitals, medical procedures and needles. Now I wondered whether it would be possible to stay in a less stressful environment and avoid hospital altogether.

Fortunately for me, the local Midwife team were very keen on homebirths and they readily agreed to attend me at home on two conditions - that my pregnancy progressed normally and that I made it past 37 weeks. Equipped with the information I needed, I turned to prayer, asking God for his guidance, asking him to steer me away from this idea if it would cause any harm to the baby. In response, God gave me the vital inner peace I needed, so I continued to pursue my aim. When, backed up by Jeremy, we revealed our plan to the Consultant at the Hospital on our last visit there at 34 weeks, we met with the expected disapproval. He sternly pointed out the risks, emphasising the danger of me bleeding to death if my Caesarean scar split, but we were armed with the statistics and politely insisted on a home birth anyway. As we left, I realised that by contrast, the real dangers of Caesarean section had never been presented to us in such a forceful way.

Having won our battle, we were free to go ahead. The head of the local Midwife team visited us at home to talk us through the whole thing, pointing out that there would be an ambulance on standby throughout, which was very reassuring. She also filled us in on the standard hospital procedures for a woman with a previous history of Caesarean section that I would be missing. Since these involved having four needles stuck into me as soon as I arrived and being linked straight to a continuous fetal monitoring machine, I felt even more glad I had opted for a homebirth. It seemed to me that the chances of achieving a natural birth with all of that tortuous gear attached were very slim indeed. One of the most positive aspects of homebirth was that I would be attended by midwives I knew throughout, who would even accompany me to hospital should the need arise. Either way, I was happy. I had won for myself the chance to give birth the way I wanted to, and knew that I would be well looked after even if things didn't go according to plan. All that was left was to wait and pray, which I did with the aid of my faithful prayer team.

10ᵗʰ January, 2008 Our baby is due in 10 days time!! This pregnancy has been great, which is more than I could ever have hoped for. I braced myself for sickness and depression and I have been given just the opposite, a time of true contentment. The end of the pregnancy has been a bit uncomfortable, but absolutely nothing compared to carrying twins. Just before Christmas my hips started to ache at night making sleep difficult. I wake many times a night in discomfort, but it doesn't at all matter when there are only a few weeks to go. Last time, I had to endure these discomforts for 4 months. No wonder I could barely drag myself through a day.

I have been truly blessed by this pregnancy. I am so grateful, because somehow it neutralises the traumatic memories from last time. I know now that it is possible for me carry a child without it being a terrible struggle. It's been lovely to feel the baby moving about inside me, to enjoy other people's attention, to feel real excitement and share it with Jeremy and the girls. Far from counting the hours till the end of it, I haven't actually wanted it to pass too quickly!

I also know that whatever is to come, maybe a difficult birth, trouble breastfeeding, or who knows what, Jesus will help me through like He has done all along.

14

Our house rearrangements to make room for the baby were all finished about a week before my due date, so we were able to spend that last week taking it easy. Every night, Kay insisted we pray that the baby would come as she was desperate to meet it! I hadn't been able to get the girls on my knee for a while, but Hattie had enjoyed using my bump as a pillow!! I made time to enjoy the feeling of the baby moving inside me, knowing that it would be the last time I had that experience. I attended my usual coffee and Bible study groups, with a prearranged agreement in place that if labour began, one of the members would drive me straight home rather than ring for an ambulance. I was afraid of ending up in hospital and then having to battle my way back out again.

My due date came and went and I began to feel nervous. I got down on my knees (no easy task!) several times to ask God for His help in bringing labour on before the medical professionals started hassling me about being induced. I remember drifting into a strange psychological state of not actually believing that the baby was *ever* going to arrive and a certainty that my body would have no idea what to do even if it did. The day after my due date, I came home from the school run and decided that I felt energetic enough to tackle a little vacuuming for the first time in ages. I started on the lounge and somehow just kept going for most of the morning, using an unexpected supply of energy that I hadn't had for weeks past. I wondered whether this was 'nesting', but I wasn't really sure.

The next day Mum and I drove over the hills to Ledbury. Mum aimed for all of the bumpiest bits of the road in an attempt to kick start labour! That evening we hosted Housegroup and I asked them to pray that the baby would arrive very soon. As they prayed, I had a sudden sure sense that their prayers would be answered. Sure enough, at 1.30 a.m. that night I was woken up by an unusual feeling, my tummy muscles tightening regularly. Just before 3 a.m., I started to bleed a little, which confirmed that things really were underway. We decided to move the girls over to their Gran and Grandad's before our home became a maternity unit. They were very excited by their middle of the night experience!

I sent texts to my prayer team and then waited for events to unroll. A few hours later, my waters broke. We informed the Midwives, who paid a brief visit, but the morning wore away with no real change and I began to feel anxious about what would happen if I didn't progress well at home. Then the Midwife rang to say that they wanted me to go into hospital at 3.30 p.m. to get a prescription for antibiotics because my broken waters brought a risk of infection. We agreed, but I was worried that if we went into hospital and labour commenced while I was there, I wouldn't be able to cope with the journey home again and would then have to face the battle over the unnecessary needles and monitoring anyway.

However, we had a few hours in hand in which to encourage labour, so we worked through everything the NCT information sheet had to suggest. Midday arrived and no labour, so I rang the prayer team for extra help. I found out later that one of my friends hijacked lunchtime prayers at Church, so a whole group of people prayed for me. But after lunch the contractions were further apart and the time when we had to set off for the hospital crept closer. Then, with only 20 minutes to spare, I was hit by a contraction of unmistakeable strength. Clutching the kitchen table, I gasped to Jeremy to call the Midwives. We were back in business for a homebirth!

From then on I had no breathing space between contractions and my TENS machine offered little more than a zappy distraction from the pain. The first Midwife arrived and calmly inspected me as I knelt in the bathroom leaning over the edge of the bath gripping Jeremy's hand. Hours passed and I remember thinking about an epidural, but the knowledge that I would have to endure contractions in a bumpy ambulance all the way to hospital bolstered my decision to stick it out at home. I didn't want gas and air in case it made me feel sick, so I just endured. I remember wondering how on earth my Great-grandmother managed to go through this *twelve* times! What a heroine.

Then I felt the incredible sensation of the baby descending and turning, so the Midwife called for another member of her team and suggested we move into our bedroom where there was more room. My body seemd to be doing a pushing thing all by itself and it took me a while to realise that instead of just observing, I was actually required to put some effort in to get the job done. I was exhausted and had another fleeting thought of hospital, but in the end I summoned my strength and pushed with all my might. With that effort, the baby was born and lifted straight up onto my chest. I was the first to hold her. It was 9.42 p.m. on 23rd January, 2007 and I had successfully survived a whole labour at home. The reward lay on my chest, perfect, alert and ready for her first feed. Elizabeth Grace, to be known as Bessy, had lots of dark hair and was utterly beautiful. As I held her, I thought with deep satisfaction, "Job done. Our family is complete."

I had torn pretty badly pushing her out and the Midwives regretfully said I had to go into hospital to be stitched up, but I was floating on a cloud of total elation and they could have told me I needed a limb amputated for all I cared. I had my baby. Bessy was cleaned up, weighed (8lbs 2oz) and popped in her car seat. I staggered to the ambulance and was strapped in, smiling. I gazed at her, grinning, all the way to hospital. There she was, my baby girl, born at home as nature intended. I felt utterly blessed.

I was operated on under a Spinal block at 1 a.m., smiling at the medical team throughout, while Jeremy cuddled Bessy nearby. I had to stay in overnight in the end, but I didn't mind. I lay and gazed at Bessy, overwhelmed by love for her, until a midwife tucked her in bed with me and then I simply fed her whenever she cried. Yes, I was reeling from the shock of childbirth pain, laying with tubes attached in an unhomely hospital bed and feeling a desperation to get back to Hattie and Kay, but underlying it all was the most intense feeling of satisfaction. I didn't sleep much that night!

Breastfeeding was the last issue that still haunted me from the past. As soon as we returned home the next day I called the NCT Breastfeeding Counsellor, intent on accepting only one person's advice instead of the piecemeal help I had received before. How simple it already seemed with only one baby to feed! Before she came, we had an exciting meeting to witness! Mum and Dad brought Hattie and Kay home from school and they greeted their little sister for the first time. They seemed a bit overawed at first, but were soon demanding their turn to hold her! I was deeply glad to see them as they breathed normality back into the house. We immediately plunged back into the usual routine, with baby Bessy accompanying us through it all. Life with three children began at last.

The Breastfeeding Counsellor arrived that evening and after an hour of her time we didn't look back. Bessy fed well, my milk came in after just two days and I actually experienced very little discomfort. I loved feeding her and what with her wriggling about and generally requiring both my hands to deal with, I found that the experience once again helped me to forgive myself for failing to feed two babies the first time round. I found it vastly easier than bottlefeeding. There was no preparation, no sterilising, no warming up, no guessing how much milk she wanted, no worrying if she hadn't taken a certain amount and no working out how much to take with us when going out. It left me with a hand free to hold a book to read to Hattie and Kay, or feed myself my lunch or hold a phone so I could chat while feeding and I could also feed Bessy while wandering around supervising the older two at bedtime. Best of all, I found it such a close, bonding experience.

Of course, it wasn't all plain sailing. Along with the milk came the baby blues, when my mood of elation finally crashed back down to earth. I stood in the shower sobbing because I couldn't work out how to be the same Mum to Hattie and Kay as I had always been while also giving Bessy everything she needed. But because I expected the emotional shift this time, I was able to relax and almost enjoy the sense of release after the momentous experiences of the previous week. The months passed in an exhausted blur. Early worries over Bessy's lack of weight gain, which made me a target for accusations of insufficient milk from the Health Visitors, were eventually resolved with a diagnosis of reflux. Once we had medicine to prevent her feed coming back up, she quickly gained weight, and, ironically, while researching the condition I discovered that one of the best treatments for baby reflux is breastfeeding, further bolstering my resolve to stick with the natural stuff. In fact, I fed her myself for more than two years and found the whole experience extremely fulfilling.

As I had hoped, my anxiety over the large age gap faded very quickly as I watched Hattie and Kay relating to their little sister. They were just lovely with her, so desperate to mother her that I came to see how lucky Bessy was to have a devoted team around her! Neither of them have ever shown the slightest sign of jealousy of Bessy, perhaps because, being twins, they have always had to share our time, attention and resources. For her part, as she grew older, Bessy altered our family dynamic in brilliant ways, providing her sisters with an adoring and ever-willing playmate, of particular use when they fell out with each other, as they frequently did. She was also the most good-natured toddler I had ever met, able to clear family tension with her infectious laugh and even giggle her way out of her own tantrums! To my delight, I had not only gained a sense of completeness but also of release. After so many years trying to conceive I could at last relax and enjoy my children without longing for more or worrying about what else I would have to endure to get them. My path may have led me through shadowy valleys but at last I had reached the green pastures the Psalm spoke of.

One day when Bessy was about 17 months old, I went into her bedroom in the morning to find that she had escaped her sleeping bag and was standing at the end of her cot holding out her arms to me. As I bent forward to lift her out, something clicked into place. Another vision had come true. Bessy's usual habit was to remain laying down in her sleeping bag, demanding our attention by singing or calling for me. That occasion was, in fact, the only one on which I found her standing at the end of the cot, seeing in the flesh the picture I had seen in my mind all those years ago.

The final vision, of me walking with one child along the common, came true several months later. Hattie and Kay were away on their first Brownie Pack Holiday, Jeremy was busy and Bessy and I had a Saturday afternoon to fill. I decided to walk with her to the nearest pond to see if there were any ducks. We strolled up the common together in the sunshine and I remembered the vision, but thought that this might not be the moment for fulfilment as the child in the vision had been holding my left hand and Bessy was clinging tightly to my right. Just at that moment, Bessy let go of my hand, ran across in front of me and took my left hand and there we were, living out the vision. We found the pond devoid of ducks, so our expedition wasn't repeated, but that day I walked back praising God for giving me such encouragement and for keeping His promises faithfully.

Despite my sense of completion, for many years I was unable to bring myself to sign the piece of paper instructing the Priory Hospital staff to remove our remaining embryos from the freezer. It cost me so much to create them that I found it hard to let them go. But by the time the permitted five years of storage were up, I discovered I was ready for the saga to draw to a close. The embryos are all gone now and our dealings with the Fertility Centre over.

I have learned so much during our decade of fertility problems. As a Christian I have found that when everything is going well it is so easy to forget to talk to God, to give in to the demands of the world and to drift far away from Him. I have known many fallow times like this. For that reason, I now see the hard experiences related in this book as blessed times because my helplessness and need made me reach out for God and in doing so I experienced the love and faithfulness of His response. I wouldn't wish infertility or depression on anyone, but they have made me the person I am, a woman who has seen that God can bring good out of anything.

I have also learned that faith need not exist in opposition to science. What is science but another way to worship God, glorying in our discoveries of the intricacy of his creation, stretching and exploring the incredible brains He created for our use? As Christians we can take delight as more and more of the supreme intelligence, creative power and mightiness of God is revealed through science, but we also need to hang on to Bible teaching as we ponder how to use our discoveries. At the beginning of my journey through infertility I was sure that the scientific route to a solution was utterly wrong. God Himself convinced me otherwise.

The birth of Hattie and Kay brought me great joy from the sheer wonder of them and from my deliverance from childlessness. The birth of Bessy brought me immense contentment from the enjoyment of her and from my sense of completion. God bore with my selfishness, my petulance, my pride and my narrowmindedness and guided me with patience and gentle encouragement throughout. Through modern medicine, through family and Church family, through direct intervention, God gave us all we needed to get through those hard years until the issue of infertility was finally behind us.

ABOUT THE AUTHOR

Rebecca Baxter lives in Worcestershire with
her husband Jeremy and daughters Hattie, Kay and Bessy.
She is a full-time mother, part-time Scout Leader,
back garden hen keeper and writes in any spare moments she can find.

Printed in Great Britain
by Amazon

78939212R00068